The Daily Daily

The Daily Daily

Nicolás Guillén

Translated, with

an Introduction by

Vera M. Kutzinski

University of California Press

Berkeley. Los Angeles. London

University of California Press
Berkeley and Los Angeles, California

University of California Press, Ltd.
London, England

Original Spanish text copyright Nicolás Guillén, reprinted by
permission of CENDA, Cuban National Center for Authors'
Rights, Havana.

Library of Congress Cataloging-in-Publication Data
Guillén, Nicolás, 1902–
    [Diario que a diario. English]
    The daily daily / Nicolás Guillén; translated, with an
introduction by Vera M. Kutzinski.
        p.   cm.
    Translation of: El diario que a diario.
    ISBN: 0-520-06218-3 (alk. paper)
    1. Cuba—Poetry. I. Kutzinski, Vera M., 1956– . II. Title.
PQ7389.G84D513 1989
861—dc19   88-29544
                                                                  CIP

Printed in the United States of America

1   2   3   4   5   6   7   8   9

Translator's Introduction

NICOLÁS GUILLÉN was born in Camagüey, Cuba, on July 10, 1902, less than two months after the ratification of the Platt amendment, which drastically qualified the terms of Cuba's recent national independence by granting the United States the right to intervene directly in its political affairs. The near coincidence of these two events, both of crucial importance to Cuban history and literature, offers a good starting point for introducing or, better, reintroducing to a North American readership a poet who has always been outspoken and unrelenting in his criticisms of the effects the United States has had on all areas and aspects of Cuban life, political, social, economic, and cultural. Such a reintroduction—reintroduction because Guillén is not entirely unknown in this country—may be a somewhat precarious endeavor; but it is, at the same time, a necessary one because Guillén's poetic achievement is frequently misrepresented by critics with an almost exclusive concern for overt political pronouncements.[1]

Guillén is usually presented as an avowed Marxist and a political nationalist. A member of Cuba's Communist party since 1937, he has been a close friend and associate of prominent figures such as Ernesto "Che" Guevara and Raúl and Fidel Castro. More recently, in addition to being Cuba's "national poet" and president of the National Union of Writers and Artists (UNEAC), he has served as deputy to the National Assembly and member of the Central Committee of the Communist party of Cuba.[2] While these biographical data are incontrovertible, they do not justify Guillén's reputation as one of the greatest living poets in the Hispanic world since Rubén Darío or Pablo Neruda. Nor do his political allegiances explain the conspicuous discrepancies between the posture he adopts in journalistic essays, speeches, and interviews and the posture that characterizes much of his poetry. The existence of such incongruities makes it problematic to use Guillén's journalistic prose—such as the essays collected in the three volumes of *Prosa de Prisa* (Fleeting Prose; 1975–76) and in *Sol de domingo* (Sunday's Sun; 1982)—as a reliable guide to his poetry. As Guillén himself offers little, if anything, that would help resolve those contradictions, the only fruitful alternative is to turn to his poetry and experience its diversity and complexity without yielding to the temptation of reducing that complexity to a singular, unambiguous message.

El diario que a diario, first published in 1972,[3] is a poem that, perhaps more aggressively than Guillén's earlier works, demands to be read in a way that goes beyond the search for overt political themes, to which so-called social poetry has traditionally been subjected. My own reading, in this particular instance, takes the form of a translation, but that translation is only one of many possible readings of this lengthy and intricate poem. What makes *El diario* so difficult, more difficult in fact that it would seem at first glance, is the very ambitiousness and scope of Guillén's poetic project: he attempts to do nothing less than present his version of Cuban history, from the colonial period to the present or, more accurately, to 1959, the year of the triumph of the Cuban Revolution. This same year also marked the end of Guillén's period of exile. After having been arrested several times for his anti-Batista activities in the early 1950s, he left Cuba in 1953, two months prior to Castro's attack on the Moncada Barracks, to live in Chile, Paris, and then Buenos Aires.

Strictly speaking, then, the postrevolutionary period is absent from *El diario*'s broad historical sweep, but its presence is felt throughout the poem in subtler and often quite unexpected ways. As its title's frank allusion to Columbus's *Diario*, the journals of his voyages to the New World, already suggests, *El diario* is a chronicle of Cuban history as well as, by extension, of American history. But it is not so much a record of the sequence of the major events that shaped Cuban history, despite the semblance of chronology that loosely joins the poem's five sections, as it is a record of Guillén's return to Cuba and, more specifically, to the history of Cuban literature, a return characterized by the intention to rediscover, revise, and rewrite that history from a postrevolutionary perspective. The question, then, is, What is the significance of this both personal and rhetorical gesture, this return to the origins of Cuban history and culture? What are its implications for Guillén's earlier, prerevolutionary works that are unquestionably part of the history *El diario* proposes to revise? And, finally, what are its implications for Cuban literature, particularly for the contemporary context into which this work inserts itself? In short, how does *El diario* affect our view both of Guillén's literary canon and of Cuba's contemporary literary scene?

I do not attempt here to offer conclusive answers to those questions; even if that were possible in each case, it would far exceed the limits (and the purpose) of this introduction. Instead, I discuss some of the issues these questions raise, hoping in the process to give readers, especially those who may be unfamiliar with Cuban literary and cultural history, sufficient information to see this poem as something more than an isolated poetic text, and a rather eccentric one at that. My hope is also to spark more of an interest in Guillén's late works, which have been neglected in favor of his early "Afro-Cuban" poems that appeared in *Motivos de son* (1930), *Sóngoro cosongo: Poemas mulatos* (1931), and *West Indies, Ltd.* (1934).

Most of the poems from these three collections have been translated into English at least once. So have a considerable number of poems from later collections such as *Cantos para soldados y sones para turistas* (Songs for Soldiers and *Sones* for Tourists; 1937), *El son entero* (The Whole *Son*; 1947), *La paloma de vuelo popular: Elegías* (The Dove of Popular Flight: Elegies; 1958), *Tengo* (I Have; 1964), *El gran zoo* (The Great Zoo; 1967), and *La rueda dentada* (The Gear; 1972).[4] The first, and so far best, translations of Guillén's early poetry were done by Langston Hughes in collaboration with Ben Frederic Carruthers and collected in a volume entitled *Cuba Libre: Poems by Nicolás Guillén* (1948). Unfortunately, only five hundred copies of this limited edition were printed, so that these translations have not been available for many years. In his introduction to *Cuba Libre*, Carruthers presents Guillén as "a spokesman for the mulatto millions of the New World," a poet who combines "the classic traditions of part of his ancestry, the Spanish, with the pronounced rhythms of Africa." He also credits Guillén with starting "a movement known as Afro-Cuban poetry," which, although somewhat inaccurate since this credit more properly belongs to Alejo Carpentier, nevertheless correctly identifies Guillén as a poet with a keen interest in the Afro-American component of Hispanic-Caribbean culture.

In fact, almost all aspects of Guillén's poetry, formal and thematic, are deeply rooted in the cross-cultural imagination of the Caribbean—*mestizaje*, as he himself calls it—and the adamant resistance to any kind of ideological dogmatism, which characterizes his best poems from the beginning of his career right up to *El diario*, is an essential part of that historical legacy. It is precisely this historically based challenge to repressive political authority, whether in the form of Spanish colonialism, United States imperialism, or even Cuban communism, that distinguishes Guillén the poet from Guillén the Communist functionary. However, very little attention has been paid to the imaginative historical dimensions of Guillén's poetry and to the way in which it lends substance to, and thus strengthens, his aggressive anti-imperialistic stance by calling for true artistic and ideological freedom. Guillén's poetry may be social poetry insofar as it is frequently concerned with concrete social and political issues; but it is not simply political propaganda naively seeking to substitute one ideological system of beliefs and values for another. What prevents his poems from falling into this latter category is their unquestionable commitment to history. Guillén's poems are permeated by an awareness of history so intense that it almost inevitably qualifies what may appear to be even the most blatant political statements by inserting them into a historical and cultural framework that relativizes them.

For Guillén, history is much more than simply a chronology of dates and events; it is a process to be created and re-created by the poet's imagination. His sense of Cuban (and Caribbean) history has everything to do with his embrace of Afro-American culture. As he insists in his "Prologue" to *Sóngoro cosongo*, "The African injection in [Cuba] is so profound, and in our well-irrigated social hydrography so many bloodlines crisscross that one would have to be a miniaturist to unravel that hieroglyph."[5] In a way, Guillén is that miniaturist who seeks to unravel the many different threads woven together in the fabric of Cuban culture. Each of his poems, in this sense, is an inscription of the very complex hieroglyphics of cross-cultural exchange: mestizaje, or what Fernando Ortiz called *transculturación*.[6]

A mulatto raised in a family that belonged to Cuba's "pequeña burguesía negra," Guillén quite literally stands at the crossroads of at least two different cultures: African and Hispanic. It is not surprising, therefore, that the great Spanish poet Federico García Lorca should have called Cuba "the land of Nicolás Guillén." Guillén's poems explore the literary potential of that mixed cultural heritage in all its intricacies and subtleties. This is particularly evident in the early *poesía negra* or *poesía mulata* of *Motivos de son*, *Sóngoro cosongo*, and also *West Indies, Ltd.*

The first two volumes, in particular, are generally considered part of the Afro-Antillean movement that began to flourish in Cuba and other parts of the Caribbean during the mid- to late 1920s. Europe's "rediscovery" of African and Afro-American cultures, ironically initiated by Oswald Spengler's influential book *The Decline of the West* (1918–1922), spurred among Latin American writers and intellectuals a strong interest in the non-Western origins of their own cultures. In Cuba, this preoccupation with cultural origins was significantly reinforced by the growing opposition to United States imperialism and the concomitant need to define a separate national identity. The Afro-Antillean movement roughly coincided with the Harlem Renaissance in the United States, Indigenism in Haiti, and the early beginnings of the Négritude movement launched in Paris in the 1930s. Among the group that constituted the Afro-Antillean movement were novelist-to-be Alejo Carpentier, Puerto Rican poet Luis Palés Matos, and lesser known Cuban poets such as Emilio Ballagas, Ramón Güirao, and José Zacarías Tallet. All of them were profoundly influenced by the ethnographic and anthropological work of Fernando Ortiz and, later, Lydia Cabrera. Interestingly enough, Guillén was the only black member of that group, unless one were to include Wifredo Lam, the Cuban painter, who was also part Chinese.

Guillén's major contribution to Cuba's search for a national identity was the *poema-son* [*son*-poem]. *Motivos de son*, a collection of eight short poems written in black Cuban vernacular first published on April 20, 1930, provoked a stir in Cuban literary circles which remains unparalleled: For the most part, their reception was favorable and even enthusiastic; yet many of Guillén's contemporaries were disturbed by the aesthetic and social implications of his poetic use of the *son*, a popular musical form. There is no doubt that Guillén's poemas-son were a daring literary experiment. They not only called attention to racial prejudice and economic injustices but also put aside conventional poetic forms in favor of the *son*, a bold gesture that in itself made a powerful symbolic statement about Cuban culture and literature.

The *son* is a formal synthesis of the Spanish, African, and *taíno* (Arawak) cultures gathered in the Caribbean. It combines fifteenth- and sixteenth-century Spanish *romance* or ballad lines with a responsorial structure that is not only African but also probably derives from the *areíto*, an Arawak celebration whose name means "dancing to remember." The earliest known *son* is the legendary "Son de la Ma Teodora," presumed to have been composed and performed by Teodora Ginés, a black Dominican, around 1580.[7] It is clear, then, that the *son*, popularized in the 1920s and 1930s by the famous Trio Matamoros and others, embodied Cuba's mixed cultural origins, calling attention particularly to the "African injection." It is perhaps not surprising that Guillén's thematic and formal emphasis on Afro-Cuban culture as a vital factor in that search for a national identity was upsetting, if not offensive, to some of his contemporaries. As he proclaims in the poem "Llegada" (Arrival), which opens his second collection, *Sóngoro cosongo*, "We [the African slaves and their descendants] bring / our features to America's definitive profile."

The poems in *Motivos de son* and *Sóngoro cosongo* also, quite subtly, reach back to the tradition of the nineteenth-century Cuban antislavery novel, extending that tradition to encompass modern cultural and political imperialism, especially on the part of the United States, the "yanqui." The struggle against imperialism in its many guises, against the imposition of one culture on another, was to become the main theme of Guillén's poetry. It rises to distinct prominence as early as *West Indies, Ltd.* and reaches entirely new proportions in *El diario*.

West Indies, Ltd. occupies a central place in Guillén's canon because it contains in embryo all the major forms and themes elaborated in his later poems. In its pan-Caribbean thrust, *West Indies, Ltd.* broadens the scope of Guillén's previous poems, a thematic development with important formal consequences. In the title poem, "West Indies, Ltd.," Guillén for the first time explores the possibilities of the long poem as a collage of many different poetic forms. This development continues in the *Elegías*, whose most daring example, the "Elegía a Jesús Menéndez" (Elegy for Jesús Menéndez), already begins to extend Guillén's formal repertoire by including so-called nonliterary discourse (e.g., newspaper headlines). This tendency to incorporate into poetry both literary and nonliterary forms culminates in *El diario*, this curious hybrid between a historical chronicle and a newspaper which compresses into its text an impressive variety of cultural and literary elements from the different traditions that come together in the Caribbean.

One poem in *West Indies, Ltd.* is of special importance to Guillén's canon in that it not only encapsulates the major issues and tensions with which Guillén will be preoccupied throughout his literary career but also demonstrates how poetic structures can modify social and political ones. I am referring to "Sensemayá: Canto para matar una culebra" (Sensemayá: Chant for Killing a Snake), which is probably Guillén's best-known poem.[8] This relatively brief work is a masterful example of the way Afro-American culture, with its long history of resistance to white hegemony, supplies important paradigms for Guillén's literary battle against modern forms of imperialism. As my previous reference to the link between *Motivos de son* and the nineteenth-century Cuban antislavery novel already suggests, Guillén frequently compares the tensions between the Antilles and the "colossus of the North" to the historical relationship between black slaves and white masters. "Sensemayá" avails itself of that analogy to explore possibilities for challenging existing power structures. More specifically, it uses the traditional Afro-Cuban festival of the "Día de Reyes" (the Day of Kings, which used to be celebrated in colonial Cuba on the day of the Epiphany) as a model for resisting authority by subverting it. In colonial Cuba, the carnivalesque festivities of the Día de Reyes brought about a momentary suspension, if not reversal, of existing power structures: the black slaves were freed symbolically for that day and allowed to celebrate their own cultural rituals and worship their own gods. In this sense, the Día de Reyes was an institution that allowed the slaves to maintain their cultural traditions. Significantly, these annual celebrations were banned in the nineteenth century. For

Guillén, the Día de Reyes carnival, much like the *son*, is a metonym of Cuban culture. It is one of the historical foundations of Cuba's national identity, which now serves Guillén to subvert the North American influences that threaten that identity.

The true importance of "Sensemayá" thus goes far beyond its skillful reproduction of a part of Afro-Cuban folklore, complete with the wonderfully resonant rhythms that seem to have become Guillén's poetic trademark. What this poem emphasizes is that poetic form and rhythm, the unusual meter so many of Guillén's readers have admired, have concrete historical dimensions. Guillén is a poet far too conscious of the historical and ideological significances of both literary and nonliterary forms, as well as far too knowledgeable of Spanish and Latin American cultural and literary history, to use such forms for purely aesthetic purposes. There is much more to Guillén's early poetry than the attempt to capture the beauty and spirit of popular poetry and oral performance.[9]

This is precisely one of the main lessons we derive from reading *El diario que a diario*, a poem that seems shockingly devoid of the compelling rhythms and the often lyrical qualities of Guillén's early work. *El diario* appears at times so dissonant and so disjointed that one begins to doubt that this text is poetry at all. One wonders, in fact, what exactly this text is. Certainly, compared to Guillén's early poems, many of which were put to music,[10] *El diario* is a text that even resists being read aloud. To anyone familiar with modern and contemporary poetry, this is, of course, nothing particularly unusual. Within an American or New World context, *El diario*, in this respect, recalls certain "experimental" poems by e.e. cummings and Octavio Paz or is perhaps even more readily reminiscent of William Carlos Williams's *Paterson*, Charles Olson's *Maximus Poems*,

Eliot's *Waste Land*, and especially Pound's *Cantos*. I am using these works as reference points, not to suggest any kind of direct literary influence they may have exerted on Guillén, whose lack of fluency in English does not permit such speculation. A number of works come to mind when searching Latin American literary history for possible precursors, but none of them are poetic texts. For instance, Alejo Carpentier's *¡Ecue Yamba-O!* (1933), Guillermo Cabrera Infante's *Tres tristes tigres* (*Three Trapped Tigers*; 1968), Miguel Barnet's *Biografía de un cimarrón* (*Autobiography of a Runaway Slave*; 1966), and even Severo Sarduy's early novels, such as *De donde son los cantantes* (*From Cuba with a Song*; 1967), seem to find resonances in *El diario*. So, for that matter, does Gabriel García Márquez's *One Hundred Years of Solitude*. Another possibility is the Nicaraguan poet Ernesto Cardenal, but Cardenal, if we keep our chronology straight, is much more influenced by Guillén, especially by his early long poems and also by the *Elegías*, than vice versa. All this leads to the conclusion that there really is no model for *El diario* in modern Latin American poetry; if anything, Guillén's poem has much more in common with the modern Latin American novel.[11]

While *El diario* may seem eclectic even within the narrower boundaries of Guillén's own poetic canon, it is in many ways a logical extension of his previous work, albeit perhaps an unexpected one for many readers. It has been suggested that *El diario* weds Guillén's poetic aspirations with his journalistic interests, much like *Sol de domingo*, a volume of earlier, unpublished prose and poetry which Guillén collected for his eightieth birthday in 1982. However, such a view returns to the biographical fallacy so typical of Guillén criticism—seeking to invest *El diario* with a false sense of unity by disregarding the contradictions between Guillén's journalistic and poetic postures. It is far more helpful to re-alize that *El diario* resists traditional ideas of unity and order, which is already evident from Guillén's intro-duction to the poem's first edition (UNEAC, 1972), un-fortunately omitted from later reprints. Guillén writes:

> Since the beginning of our history, from the final glow of the fifteenth century to the second half of the twentieth century where we are now, four centuries have elapsed in which Cuba has consecutively been trading post, colony (with two rebellions against Spain and the brief period of British rule), republic under the Yankee's protectorate, and finally Revo-lution. In order not to write either a *textbook* or an epic poem, I have used a series of scenes in which this process culminated, alluding to them in a style that seeks to be cine-matographic, journalistic, vibrant, suggestive. *To suggest* is all this little book aspires to. And is not suggestiveness per-haps the most direct language poetry has?[12]

In other words, *El diario* is neither a textbook of sorts, narrating historic events in chronological se-quence, nor an epic detailing heroic feats. Instead, it is a poem that draws attention to items that fall through the cracks of what may be called official histories (both the textbook and the epic belong to that category). In this respect, *El diario* resembles Juan Rodríguez Freyle's *El carnero* (1636), a highly unusual chronicle of the Kingdom of New Granada, not so much in style but certainly in intent and effect. What Guillén, above all, emphasizes is the vital connection between history and language. History, in *El diario*, is a vast assemblage of texts and fragments of texts, each characterized by its form and style, that is, by the rhetorical conventions of which it avails itself. These conventions, literary or not, identify each text, each fragment with a specific historical setting. Each historical period, like each cul-tural tradition, has its own forms of discourse, its own peculiar language. History, then, assumes the shape of a gigantic archive filled with all kinds of different texts representing a multitude of historical and literary events.

It is this notion of history as an archive that Guillén explores in *El diario*. I have noted before that the poem closes with an allusion to the triumph of the Cuban Revolution in 1959, which is also an allusion to the end of Guillén's exile. Insofar as *El diario* is the product of Guillén's return to Cuba, that return is equivalent to an immersion in history and thus to a journey of a different kind—a journey into the archives of memory whose doors had been pushed wide open by the revolution. We find in this idea of return and revolution Guillén's definition of intellectual and artistic freedom: the freedom to hold inventory of the past, which, for him, is a process of artistic creation, of *invention*. The product of Guillén's double venture, invention and inventory, *El diario* becomes a gathering of the most diverse and unusual texts: public ordinances; newspaper advertisements for restaurants, funeral homes, artwork, bullfights, books, pamphlets, plays, dromedaries, prophylactics, perfumes, pills, potions, smiles, and slaves; society news items; editorials; headlines; shipping lists; and clippings of all sorts. It is no coincidence that this list reads very much like what we find in the item entitled "La quincalla del ñato." *El diario* is, after all, a storehouse of very strange things. In this regard, it recalls *El gran zoo* (1967), Guillén's New World bestiary, with its display of all sorts of fabulous species ranging from "The Hunger" to tigers, eagles and the "KKK."

What *El diario* also shares with *El gran zoo* is not just its acerbic satire and exquisite humor but also, more important, a return to the chronicles of the Indies as a literary origin. If the chronicles, embodying the confrontation of the European literary imagination with the new and unfamiliar surroundings of the New World, contain the early beginnings of what Carpentier was to call "lo real maravilloso americano," the marvelous American reality, then their significance to Guillén's persistent emphasis on Cuba's mixed cultural (and literary) origins is quite clear. Latin American writers from Alejo Carpentier to Gabriel García Márquez and the late Borges to Carlos Fuentes have identified the chronicles of the Indies as crucial sources of the modern Latin American novel. *El gran zoo* and *El diario* to an even greater extent also establish the chronicles' importance to twentieth-century Latin American poetry and thus continue one of the legacies of Neruda's *Canto general*, but in unique ways.

Cultural interaction becomes in *El diario* a lively exchange of literary and nonliterary forms and genres—as in the "Son de la Ma Teodora" and in Guillén's own poemas-son—which ultimately results in a kind of "stylelessness." This stylelessness is not so much characterized by an absence of style as by an overabundance, a promiscuous cohabitation of different styles and forms from many historical periods in the same cultural (and textual) space. This seemingly chaotic stylelessness, whether in Havana's architecture, in Cuban music, or in literature, is an important formal manifestation of Guillén's idea of mestizaje. It is also a salient feature of the Latin American neobaroque, and in a sense we may say that *El diario* offers us a poetic version of Carpentier's *Concierto barroco* (Baroque Concert; 1974). Much like Carpentier's novel, Guillén's poem once again poses the question of how to bring together the different cultural traditions that are present in Cuba and the New World, how to place the dissonant sounds of African drums next to the harmonious forms of the great European masters; in other words, how to articulate the multiplicity of one's cultural origins and fashion from that multiplicity a viable cultural identity.

Guillén's answer to these questions in *El diario* can be inferred from his allusions to Afro-Cuban culture, which range from veiled references (in "Pregón Segundo") to Silvestre de Balboa's *Espejo de paciencia* (Mirror of Patience; 1608), the first Cuban poem to include a black character, to the "Anima Sola" prayer that can be found among the items assembled in the "quincalla del ñato." In fact, we discover on close scrutiny of the poem's "stock" a return to the model of Afro-Cuban carnival and its playfully subversive qualities. *El diario* is not just a poem of resistance to various forms of imperialism; it goes even further by parodying the "official" image and identity of Cuba as a culturally "white" society.

By the mid-nineteenth century, Cuba's slave population had grown so disproportionately that whites found themselves in the minority. While this was in no way an exceptional situation in the Antilles, there was one major difference between Cuba and other sugar-producing Caribbean islands: in colonial Cuba, free blacks, most of whom lived and worked in the cities, accounted for roughly one fifth of the total population. The white minority's persistent fear of losing control over the "persons of color," a category that, since the eighteenth century, included both slaves and free blacks, may well have played an important part in delaying emancipation until 1880. The fear of slave insurrections was not unfounded; unrests and revolts were frequent, having begun as early as 1677 with the successful slave revolt in the copper mines of Santiago del Prado, and the increasing suspicion that free blacks would ally themselves with freed slaves was readily confirmed by the Aponte conspiracy in 1812, a belated aftershock of the Haitian Revolution (1791–1804). Echoes of this idea of "the black peril" can even be found in the antislavery writings of José Antonio Saco and Domingo Delmonte. This paranoia led to the indiscriminate oppression of all "persons of color," which culminated in the violent reaction to the alleged conspiracy of "La Escalera" (The Ladder) in 1844. It even prevailed after slavery had been officially abolished in 1880 and explains the long period of transition—in the form of the so-called patronato—to which the former slaves were subjected before they became free wage laborers. For all intents and purposes, slavery continued in Cuba until 1886. Even after that, the former slaves largely continued to work in the cane fields, having little, if any, economic mobility. Racial tensions persisted along with economic injustices well into the twentieth century and were constantly reinforced by the influence of the United States on Cuba. Evidence of this was the murder in 1912 of a group of black veterans who protested against their unrewarded participation in the Spanish-American War and, more recently, the assassination in 1948 of Jesús Menéndez, the black union leader and close friend of Guillén's.

El diario insistently reminds us of this underside of Cuban history. Guillén emerges in *El diario* as a kind of Hermes figure whose irreverent play on language and literary conventions makes us aware of the fact that things are not at all what they seem to be, that much lies hidden behind and underneath the polished rhetorical veneer of official pronouncements and alleged historical truths. It is hardly a coincidence that the reprint of *El diario* in Guillén's *Obra poética* is preceded by the poet's drawing of a grinning devil. Neither is the fact that the sarcastic "letter" addressed to Eliseo Diego, which serves as a prologue to the poem, is a tercet composition that recalls Dante's *Commedia*. *El diario* encourages us to acknowledge that suggestiveness is indeed poetry's most direct language. And it is precisely this suggestiveness, the product of a literary imagination at the crossroads of African and European traditions, that characterizes Guillén's poetic achievement. *El diario*, ultimately, instills in its reader a healthy suspicion of language's ability directly to articulate incontrovertible truths, whether historical or political, and this suspicion is essential to reading all of Guillén's poems.

At the same time, this suspicion of language as a characteristic feature of Guillén's poetic discourse raises certain questions about the translatability of his poems in general and *El diario* in particular, especially about their translatability into English. On the one hand, there is is no doubt that these poems can be translated, in the loose sense of that term. On the other hand, the question is whether or not, and how, such translations, including this one, can move beyond the "inaccurate transmission of inessential content," a phrase Walter Benjamin used to define bad translations.[13] An example would be a translator's attempt at re-creating what he or she perceives as the "meaning" of a particular word, phrase, or text without due attention to the language of the original or, even more important, to the relationship between the language of the original and the language of the translation. Existing translations of Guillén's poems, with the possible exception of those by Hughes and Carruthers, have tended to treat his poetic language simply as a tool for the conveyance of specific political messages, thus pretending to create a likeness between the original and the translation. The fact of the matter is, however, that no translation is *like* the original on which it is based, even if we pretend that both "say," or "mean," the same thing. Even if it were possible to achieve such a likeness, the desirability of such an endeavor is questionable.

With regard to this edition, this means that any likeness suggested by certain typographical resemblances

that almost inevitably result from the bilingual juxta-
position of original and translation is highly deceptive.
All it should suggest is that there exists some sort of re-
lationship between original and translation, the nature
of which I shall attempt to clarify.

As mentioned before, *El diario* is a poem that is very
much concerned with language and, more specifically,
with the relationship between different discourses (e.g.,
literary language, bureaucratic language, the language
of advertising, etc.) as well as between different lan-
guages (Spanish, French, English). In this sense, the
poem itself already poses the question of translation
and translatability by exploring what happens when a
multiplicity of languages confront each other in the
same text. What happens are certain kinds of linguistic
transformations, changes in meaning. We may say, in
fact, that *El diario* is a poem about the effects of those
transformations on a given culture, in this case Cuba,
and about the historical significances or dimensions of
those effects. For instance, to achieve linguistic con-
trasts, Guillén uses a number of English words and
phrases in the section about American interventionism
in Cuba since 1902. The presence of these foreign
words and phrases in a Spanish text is representative of
the effects the presence of the United States had on Cu-
ban culture, that is, of an "Americanization" so intense
that it changed even Cuban Spanish. Once *El diario* is
translated into English, that linguistic contrast and
conflict disappears, and the poem's linguistic surface is
evened out in a way that makes it completely different
from the original Spanish text. Nor will it do simply to
replace an English word used in the original with a
Spanish one in the translation to maintain at least an
outward appearance of linguistic diversity. To give an
example: to substitute "espectáculo" for "show" (in
"Miami Club") or "Quien no es" for "Who's Not" (in

"Una obra que hará época") creates an effect completely different from that of the original, since the Spanish words and phrase have entirely different connotations. An additional complication is that Guillén uses English words and phrases not just to show a contamination of the Cuban lexicon but also to parody and thus subvert the cultural values and institutions they represent. A good example here is again his use of "Who's Not" instead of "Who's Who." Conversely, it is impossible to find an English word that would approximate the etymological resonances of Arabic-derived "algarabía," which means something like noisy chatter or gibberish, or to capture the precise meaning of the Cuban idiom "La quincalla del ñato." Both expressions are employed in part to suggest African elements in Cuban (and Peninsular) Spanish, which creates yet another level of linguistic and cultural subversion.

If the task or responsibility of Guillén's translator is to reproduce the effect of his use of language, that is, the process of linguistic subversion at work in *El diario*, then fidelity to the original becomes a highly ironic matter. It may be possible, perhaps, to be faithful to the poem's language, if by language we mean individual words that could be translated literally, but that kind of faithfulness stands in total opposition to the overall effect of that language. Guillén's practice of linguistic subversion is exceedingly difficult to reproduce in English, especially since English is one of the languages being subverted. This has serious implications: it means that *El diario* invalidates its English translation. In relation to the original text, such a translation constitutes an act of linguistic and cultural imposition, if not aggression. Given how *El diario* conceives of the relationship between English and Spanish, an English translation is inevitably an attempt at taking over and distorting the original. This is true of any translation, but in the case of *El diario* it is almost automatically charged with very specific historical and ideological significances: an English translation is, in and by itself, a form of cultural imperialism. For that reason, almost from the very beginning, an English translation of *El diario* is condemned to failure. But there is, after all, a difference between a translation that succeeds, in some sense at least, because it is aware of its failure and one that fails because it is not. It is with this distinction in mind that I have approached the precarious task of translating *El diario*.

■

NOTES

1. For detailed bibliographical information about Guillén's own writings and critical studies of his work, see *Bibliografía de Nicolás Guillén: Biblioteca nacional de José Martí* (Havana: Instituto Cubano del Libro, 1974). More recent studies include Nancy Morejón's *Recopilación de textos sobre Nicolás Guillén* (Havana: Casa de las Américas, 1974) and *Nación y mestizaje en Nicolás Guillén* (Havana: UNEAC, 1982); Jorge M. Ruscalleda Bercedóniz's *La poesía de Nicolás Guillén* (Río Piedras: University of Puerto Rico, 1975); Dennis Sardinha's *The Poetry of Nicolás Guillén* (London: New Beacon Books, 1976); Lorna V. Williams's *Self and Society in the Poetry of Nicolás Guillén* (Baltimore: Johns Hopkins University Press, 1982); Keith Ellis's *Cuba's Nicolás Guillén: Poetry and Ideology* (Toronto: University of Toronto Press, 1983). My own *Against the American Grain: Myth and History in William Carlos Williams, Jay Wright, and Nicolás Guillén* (Baltimore: Johns Hopkins University Press, 1987) and a special issue on Nicolás Guillén I guest edited for *Callaloo* (vol. 10, spring 1987) are attempts to revise Guillén's popular image.

2. Details about Guillén's life can be found in Angel Au-

gier's two-volume biography *Nicolás Guillén: Notas para un estudio biográfico-crítico* (Santa Clara, Cuba: Universidad Central de las Villas, 1964) and his *Nicolás Guillén* (Havana: Instituto del Libro, 1971). See also Guillén's *Paginas vueltas: Memorias* (Havana: UNEAC, 1982).

3. The first edition was published by UNEAC. A second edition appeared in 1979 (Editorial Letras Cubanas). In addition, the poem is reprinted in its entirety in *Obra poética*, vol. 2, edited by Angel Augier (Havana: Instituto Cubano del Libro), and in *Summa poética*, edited by Luis Iñigo Madrigal (Madrid: Ediciones Catedra, 1976).

4. *Man-Making Words: Selected Poems of Nicolás Guillén*, translated and annotated, with an introduction by Robert Márquez and David Arthur McMurray (Amherst: University of Massachusetts Press, 1972); *¡Patria o muerte! The Great Zoo and Other Poems by Nicolás Guillén*, translated by Robert Márquez (New York: Monthly Review Press, 1972); and *Tengo*, translated by Richard J. Carr (Detroit: Broadside Press, 1974).

5. *Obra poética*, vol. 1, 114.

6. See Fernando Ortiz's *Contrapunteo cubano del tabaco y el azúcar* (1947), translated by Harriet de Onís as *Cuban Counterpoint: Tobacco and Sugar* (New York: Random House, 1970).

7. There are well-founded doubts that this "Son," which was not transcribed and published until the nineteenth century, is an authentic product of the sixteenth century. For further information, see Odilio Urfé, "Factores que integran la música cubana," *Islas* 2 (September–December 1959): 7–21; and Alberto Muguercia Muguercia, "Teodora Ginés ¿mito o realidad histórica?" *Revista de la Biblioteca Nacional José Martí* 8 (September–December 1971): 53–85.

8. For a more substantial reading of this poem, see my *Against the American Grain*, 136–146.

9. For two excellent discussions of Guillén's early poems, see Roberto González Echevarría's "Guillén as Baroque: Meaning in *Motivos de son*," *Callaloo*, Special Issue on Nicolás Guillén, 10 (spring 1987): 302–317; and Gustavo

---

Pérez Firmat's "Nicolás Guillén Between the *Son* and the Sonnet," ibid., 318–328.

10. There is a fiftieth anniversary edition of *Motivos de son* which includes musical scores by Amadeo Roldán, Alejandro García Caturla, Eliseo Grenet, and Emilio Grenet (Havana: Editorial Letras Cubanas, 1980).

11. See my comments on *El diario* in *Against the American Grain*, 164–235.

12. Quoted in Morejón, *Nación y mestizaje en Nicolás Guillén*, 314–315; my translation.

13. "The Task of the Translator," in *Illuminations* (New York: Schocken Books, 1969), 70.

The Daily Daily

AVISOS, MENSAJES, PREGONES

Prologuillo no estrictamente necesario

Primero fui el notario
polvoriento y sin prisa,
que inventó el inventario.
Hoy hago de otra guisa:
soy el diario que a diario
te previene, te avisa
numeroso y gregario.
¿Vendes una sonrisa?
¿Compras un dromedario?
Mi gran stock[1] es vario.
Doquier[2] mi planta pisa
brota lo extraordinario.

PROBLEMAS DE PURISMO.[1] *Stock*, voz inglesa. [2] *Doquier*, arcaísmo. Mas
para nuestra empresa, todo es uno y lo mismo.

LA DIRECCIÓN

EPÍSTOLA

Al poeta Eliseo Diego

Estos viejos papeles que te envío,
esta tinta pretérita, Eliseo,
¿no moverán tu cólera o tu hastío?

Como un arroyo fácil, mi deseo
fue que tan simple historia discurriera
a tu lado fugaz. Pero ahora veo

WARNINGS, MESSAGES, ANNOUNCEMENTS

Not strictly necessary little Prologue

In the beginning I was the notary,
dust covered and in no hurry,
inventor of the inventory.
Today I play a different part:
I am the Daily that daily
forewarns you and puts you on guard,
I am numerous and friendly.
Is it a smile you are selling?
Or a dromedary you want to buy?
My large *stock*[1] has everything in ready supply.
Wheresoever[2] my foot touches the ground,
extraordinary things can be found.

PROBLEMS OF PURITY. [1] *Stock*, Anglicism. [2] *Wheresoever*, archaic. But in
our press, it is all one and the same.

THE MANAGEMENT

EPISTLE

For the poet Eliseo Diego

These old papers I am sending you,
Eliseo, this ink of a bygone day,
will they not bore you or cause dismay?

Like a plain little brook, I did pray
that so simple a story
should flow by you without worry.

que el arroyo ha inundado la pradera
y que tapando sendas y breñales
al Tínima recuerda en primavera.[1]

Con chicotes tremendos, con puñales
exigen voceando mis lectores
que me vaya a otro sitio a mear pañales.

Juro por los sinsontes y las flores
que en aquesta ocasión no he pretendido
provocar con mi verso tus furores.

Torpeza y no maldad más bien ha sido.
Mira tú cómo a veces un disparo
medido, bien medido, ultramedido,

al no dar en el blanco da en el claro,
lo que quiere decir que se va al viento,
hecho por lo demás que en mí no es raro.

Al trote femoral de mi jumento
regreso pues sobre mis propias huellas
hasta dejarlo al fin libre y contento

en campos de zafir paciendo estrellas,
(como Luis el de Góngora decía)
para (me digo yo) eructar centellas.

Te entrego mi poema. Algarabía
en lengua de piratas y bozales
donde de todo material había:

---

[1] El Tínima no llega a un mal riacho,
  mas si le llueve, es un riacho macho.

But the brook has flooded, I'm afraid,
and it covers paths and brambles,
like the Tínima on a springtime raid.[1]

With daggers and a great big quirt
my readers howl and require
that I go elsewhere to spread my dirt.

I swear by the name of mockingbirds and flowers
that this time it has not been my desire
to provoke your ire with my poetic powers.

Malicious I am not, just clumsy.
Look how at times a shot,
no matter how well aimed it may be

misses its goal but still misses not:
it shoots clear through, you see,
which happens frequently with me.

The skeletal trot of my donkey
takes me back to the steps that here brought me,
until I leave him, free and quite happy,

in sapphire fields grazing on stars
(as Luis de Góngora used to say)
in order (I tell myself) to burp up fiery chars.

I submit my poem to you. Noisy chatter
in the tongue of pirates and slaves from Africa,
where all my stuff I always gather:

---

[1] The Tínima is nothing but a sorry little creek,
  but rain brings out its aggressive streak.

No sólo los Urrutias y González,
los ya Rojas y Alonsos, los Angulos,
y en fin otros diversos animales,

sino los tristes que ponían sus culos
a que aquellos señores los patearan
con patas no de gentes, mas de mulos.

¡Con qué lágrimas duras no lloraran!
¡Con qué voz tan sangrienta no pidieran!
¡Con qué puños tan altos no se alzaran!

¡Cuántos miles y miles no cayeran!
¡Oh Reino de la Muerte, tiempo 'España,
charcos de sangre tus provincian eran!

Luego el castrón del Tío, cuya maña
usual en sus atracos de usurero
ni al sobrino más fiel turba o engaña,

salvo si el tal sobrino es un madero.
Y maderos tuvimos, es el caso.
a cual más intrigante y bandolero,

y a quienes hubo que cortar el paso
para abrirnos el nuestro hacia adelante
como el pueblo acostumbra: de un trancazo.

Dixi, buen Eliseo, ya es bastante.
Perdona alguna rima mal situada
y tenme por tu amigo el más constante.
(Tú dirás: —*Gracias, viejo*. Yo: —*De nada*.)

The Urrutias and Gonzálezes are not the only finds,
there are also the Rojas, Alonzos, and Angulos,
not to mention other strange beasts of all kinds,

and sorry figures who stick out their behinds
for those fine gentlemen to kick
with feet like hooves, not the human kind.

What bitter tears will they not cry!
With what bleeding voices will they not plead!
What hard fists will they not raise to defy!

After how many thousand miles will they not despair!
O Kingdom of Death, time of Spain,
your provinces, pools of blood they were.

Then there was this Uncle, what a thief,
whose typical cunning in his racketeering raids
even the most loyal nephew could not believe,

unless of course that nephew were a dunce.
And dunces we had plenty, if the truth be told,
each one a crook, more conniving and bold,

and we had to stop them dead in their tracks
no longer to put our future on hold,
by hitting them over the head with an axe.

Dixi, dear Eliseo, I have come to an end.
Forgive any misplaced rhymes
and regard me as your most faithful friend.
(You will say: *Thanks, old buddy*. I: *You bet*.

Hermes hermético trimesgisto,
no me hables en griego, por los Clavos de Cristo,
y dime en romance si otra cosa tan feroz has visto,
ni si nadie que no sea Mercurio,
tu igual, tu compadre, tu hermano,
que habla el latín con acento romano,
podría dar fe de este modo sutil de robar (anunciar).
Anunciar que nos quieren robar (o nos van).

El Gran Ladrón
manda dar un pregón
para saber
lo que a cada uno le puede coger.
Y otro más
contra los que se quieren coger la ciudad.

PREGÓN PRIMERO

Según que lo han de uso e costumbre,
se ayuntaron en junta e cabildo
los señores Juan Ruiz Calabaza,
Antonio el de Écija, Fernando de Azumbre,
Bernardo Rodeja, Hernán de Sucasa,
Francisco Cartucho e Pero Caramba,
e mandaron a dar un pregón
en públicas plazas e calles,
que todos declaren los cuartos
que para su uso cada uno tobiere,
e con ello se pague lo más que al servicio
del Rey combiniere.

E así se pregone.

Hermetic Hermes Trismegistus,
do not, for the sake of Christ's Nails, address me in
　　Greek,
but tell me plainly if you have ever seen anything
　　more sleek,
and if anybody but Mercury,
your peer, your brother, your companion,
who speaks Latin with a Roman inflection,
could possibly sanction this subtle practice of stealing
　　(advertising).
To announce that they plan a robbery (or that one is
　　in the making).

The Greatest Thief in all the nation
issues a public proclamation
to ascertain
what from each one he can gain.
And yet another proclamation
about the city's projected invasion.

■■■■

FIRST ORDINANCE

In accordance with custom and habit,
the honorable squires John Calabash,
Tony the Child, Ferdinand the Lush,
Thomas the Twister, Herman Homebuddy,
Frank Bigshot, and Peter the Devil,
all members of the Town Council will congregate
and order an announcement to be made
in all the streets and public places,
for everyone to declare officially
the abodes they use privately,
and that to the King each may render
the appropriate sum of legal tender.
　　　　　　　　　Be it thus announc'd.

PREGÓN SEGUNDO

Según uso e costumbre,
en reunión del Cabildo fue acordado:
Que las sendas que salen de la playa
se cierren e no haya
habitante ninguno tan osado
de las abrir, pues ha llegado aviso
de que este pueblo e villa
recuestado e robado
de piratas franceses
fue, e que por más de un punto penetraron;
si es español, so pena
de que pague mil pesos
para gastos de guerra,
o recibir azotes hasta cien
si acaso desta plata careciera;
si negra libre fuera,
o mulata tal vez o mero esclavo,
que sea desjarretado
de un pie; si fuese indio, que trabaje
en la obra del Fuerte un año entero.
Así sea pregonado, así se diga
en la plaza e las calles desta villa.

Oh tiempos iniciales
en que la vida se pagaba en pesos y en reales,
cuando no, con azotes
de fuetes que eran como calabrotes;
y de las entrepiernas de hembras baratas
caían los frutos de las rudas *cañonas,*
(cubanismo: bravatas)

SECOND ORDINANCE

In accord with custom and habit,
the Council further resolv'd:
That the dirt roads to the beach
be clos'd and that no person
be so bold
to reopen them, as word has reach'd us
that French Pirates are on their way
to sack and ravage
this town and its people,
and that they have already broken through in several
* places;*
if the offender is a Spaniard, the penalty
is a thousand pesos
for the war fund;
or up to a hundred lashes
in case that he or she doth not have enough silver;
if the offender is a free woman of color, a mulatta
* perhaps,*
or just a simple slave, she shall pay the price
of losing a foot;
if the offender is an Indian, he shall be sentenc'd to
* hard labor*
at the Fort for the duration of an entire year.
Be it thus ordain'd, be it thus proclaim'd
in the marketplace and the streets of this here town.

Oh, good old times
when life was still counted in dollars and dimes,
and if not, then at least in whiplashes
that burned like cat-o'-nine-tail gashes,
when from cheap females' crotches
the fruits of crude *canoñas*
(Cubanism: rapes)

que daban los señores en celo
bien repletos de hormonas,
en camas y tarimas, sin olvidar el suelo,
a las esclavas negras y mulatas;
tiempos en fin de cuando
la Virgen del Rosario,
amiga del vecindario,
bajaba de su altar a espantar la viruela,
cumpliendo un previsor
acuerdo extraordinario
del Cabildo reunido siempre en vela,
ojo avizor . . .

¡Santo, santo, santo!
¡No más viruela, oh Virgen, por favor!
¡Santo, santo, santo!
¡No más viruela, oh Virgen, por favor!
¡Santo, santo, santo!
¡No más viruela, oh Virgen, por favor!
¡Cúbrenos con tu manto,
no más viruela, oh Virgen, por favor!

Aviso contra la culebrilla. Según informe presentado
por el Alcalde Ordinario, una imponente festividad va
a ser hecha en honor de San Antonio Abad, por la epi-
demia o enfermedad de la culebrilla que se ha experi-
mentado en el ganado de cerda (puercos) con grave
daño para el dicho ganado. Esta festividad estará presi-
dida por el señor Dr. Don José Manuel Mayorga, Mae-
stro de Ceremonias de la pontificia y real Universidad
de San Jerónimo.

Aviso contra muertes súbitas. Se confirmó en Cabildo
reunido al efecto de la grave epidemia que se está pa-
deciendo en esta ciudad, de que se experimentan

dropped like ripe grapes,
fruits forced on black and mulatto wenches
by lords in heat
and with hormones well replete,
in beds, on the floors and on low benches!
Times, in brief, when
the Virgin of Rosario,
the neighborhood's faithful friend,
scared away the smallpox as down from her altar she
    bent,
which was quite in accordance
with the Council's exceptional vigilance;
as always in session in the wee hours of the day,
the watchful eye keeping danger at bay . . .

Oh, Holy, Holy, Holy!
Please no more smallpox, oh Virgin!
Oh, Holy, Holy, Holy!
Please no more smallpox, oh Virgin!
Oh, Holy, Holy, Holy!
Please no more smallpox, oh Virgin!
Cover us with your mantle,
please no more smallpox, oh Virgin!

Warning against hoof-and-mouth disease. According
to information released by the Mayor, a magnificent cel-
ebration will be held in honor of Abbot San Antonio
against the epidemic or disease of hoof-and-mouth
which has been found in small cloven-footed animals
(pigs) with serious damage to said animals. The festiv-
ities will be presided over by Dr. Joseph Manuel Ma-
yorga, Master of Ceremonies at the Royal and Pontifical
University of San Jeronimo.

Warning against sudden deaths. It has been confirmed
during the Council meeting called because of the effects
of the serious epidemic with which this city has been

muertes casi repentinas. Acordóse una pública rogativa por la salud común, acudiendo a la Piedad Divina para que alivie y mejore lo nocivo de estas enfermedades. Procesíon (que será muy del agrado del Señor) el segundo sábado de este mes. Se ruega aportar hachones.

OTRAS ADVERTENCIAS Y CUIDADOS ACERCA DE GRAVES MALES Y ANDANZAS QUE AFLIGEN A ESTA CIUDAD, EN LA PRÓXIMA ENTREGA EL LECTOR HALLARÁ

ESCLAVOS EUROPEOS

ADVERTENCIA IMPORTANTE

Es sorprendente la semejanza que existe entre el texto de estos anuncios y el lenguaje empleado por los traficantes en esclavos africanos (negreros) para proponer su mercancía. Forzados por la costumbre general aceptamos su publicación, no sin consignar la repugnancia que tan infame comercio produce en nuestro espíritu.

Sobre la venta y compra de esclavos, jóvenes y en perfecta salud, y también acerca de fugas de los mismos, su cambio por objetos de interés vario, así en la vida pública como familiar:

afflicted that a series of almost sudden deaths have occurred. It has been agreed to make a public plea for communal health and to ask for Divine Intervention to alleviate the damage caused by these diseases. A procession (which will please God) will be held on the second Saturday of this month. Participants are asked to bring torches.

OTHER ANNOUNCEMENTS AND WARNINGS
CONCERNING GRAVE EVILS AND
RUMINATIONS
SUCH AS AFFLICT THIS CITY
WILL APPEAR IN THE NEXT ISSUE.

<hr/>

EUROPEAN SLAVES

IMPORTANT ANNOUNCEMENT

The similarity between the text of the following announcements and the language that the traffickers in African slaves (slave traders) used to advertise their merchandise is indeed striking. Compelled by generally accepted custom we have agreed to print these notices, however not without emphasizing the repugnance with which this infamous commerce fills our spirit.

About the sale of slaves, young and in perfect health, and also about the escape of such slaves, their exchange for different kinds of objects, in public auctions and privately:

VENTAS

Véndese un blanco joven, calesero
de una o de dos bestias;
general cocinero
y más que regular repostero.
Impondrán
en casa de D. Pedro Sebastián,
al 15½ de Teniente Rey,
donde además se arrienda un buey.

Dos blancas jóvenes por su
ajuste: en la calle de Cuba
casa Nº 4 impondrán.

Blanca de cuatro meses de parida, sin un rasguño ni una
herida, de buena y abundante leche, regular lavandera,
criolla cocinera, sana y sin tacha, fresquísima mu-
chacha: EN 350 PESOS LIBRES PARA EL VEN-
DEDOR, EN LA CALLE DE LA PALOMA, AL Nº
133.

Una pareja de blanquitos, hermanos de 8 y 10 años,
macho y hembra, propios para distraer niños de su
edad. También una blanquita (virgen) de 16. En la
calle del Cuervo, al 430, darán razón y precio.

SALES

White boy for sale, can drive
one or two horses,
general cook,
and an above average confectioner.
Interested buyers should inquire
at the house of D. Pedro Sebastián,
15½ de Teniente Rey,
where an ox is also for hire.

Two white wenches for hire.
Address inquiries to the Street of Cuba,
House No. 4.

White girl who gave birth four months ago, without a
scratch or a blemish; has good and abundant milk; av-
erage washerwoman, can cook creole dishes, healthy
and flawless, very sweet girl: THE SELLER ASKS
FOR 350 PESOS LIBRES. CALLE DE LA PALO-
MA, NO. 133.

A pair of white children, brother and sister, 8 and 10
years old, can be used for entertaining children of their
own age. Also for sale a white girl (virgin) of 16. Price
and details can be obtained at the Calle de Cuervo, No.
430.

CAMBIO

Se cambia un blanco libre de tacha
por una volanta de la marca Ford
y un perro.
Casa Mortuoria de la Negra Tomasa,
junto al Callejón del Tambor
(segunda cuadra después de la plaza)
darán razón.

FUGA

Ha fugado de casa de su amo
un blanco de mediana estatura,
ojos azules y pelo colorado,
sin zapatos,
camisa de listado
sobre fondo morado.
Quien lo entregue
será gratificado.
San Miguel, 31,
estramuros,
casa que llaman del Tejado.

ACTO DE JUSTICIA

El blanco Domingo Español será conducido el viernes
próximo por las calles de la Capital llevando una navaja
colgada al cuello, misma con que causó heridas a sus
amos, un matrimonio del que era esclavo. Le darán
ciento cincuenta azotes de vergüenza pública, y cin-
cuenta más en la picota situada en la calle de este
nombre. Después que sane del látigo será enviado a
Ceuta por diez años.

EXCHANGE

Will exchange unblemished white male
for a Ford carriage
and a dog.
Funeral Home of the Negress Tomasa,
next to Drum Alley
(second block from the Plaza)
Details will be supplied.

ESCAPE

Escaped from the house of his master
has a white man of medium stature,
his eyes are blue and red is his hair,
his feet are bare,
and his shirt has stripes
on a background of purple.
Whoever returns him
will have no cause for regret.
San Miguel 31,
outskirts,
the house they call The Shed.

ACT OF JUSTICE

Next Friday the white slave Domingo Español will be
dragged through the streets of the capital carrying
around his neck the same razor with which he slashed
his masters, a couple whose slave he used to be. He will
receive one hundred fifty lashes in public and fifty more
at the whipping post in the Street Picota. After his
wounds have healed he will be sent to Ceuta for ten
years.

SONETO

La aldea es ya ciudad, mas no por ello
se piense que dejó de ser aldea:
en las calles el pueblo caga y mea
sin que el ojo se ofenda ni el resuello.

Paciencia hay que tener más que un camello
con el agua podrida y la diarrea,
y quien de noche ingenuo se pasea
a escondido puñal arriesga el cuello.

Moscas, mosquitos, ratas y ratones,
polvo hecho fango, charcas pestilentes,
fiebres malignas, chancros, purgaciones,

contagio son de bestias y de gentes,
bajo un sol de ladrones y gritones
y una luna de dientes relucientes.

INTERLUDIO[1]

(Fragmentos de poemas célebres)

Con diez coñones por bonda
vianto en pipa a toda bula,
no carta el mer, sino viula
un bularo bergantón:
Bajol pireta que lloman
por su bravara «El Temodo»,
en tido el mer conosodo
del ino al etro confón.

[1] Teda semejonza con Espronzuda es fortuota.

SONNET

The village is a city now, but don't suppose
that much has changed because of this:
in the streets people shit and piss,
without offending either eye or nose.

More patient than a camel you must be
with the foul water and the sewage slime,
and if you're dumb enough to go out at nighttime,
a hidden dagger may terminate your spree.

Flies, mosquitoes, rats, and mice,
putrid puddles, dust turned to mud,
malignant fevers, syphilis, menstrual blood,

contagious for man and beast, but no one cares
as the sun on crooks and victims glares
and the moon its sparkling teeth bares.

INTERLUDE[1]

(Fragments of famous poems)

Ormed with tun connens,
oll soils swellen in the wand
she flaus ocress the woters,
a swaft braggontan:
The Druodful Ene they coll hur,
bucouse she is so beld,
knewn oll ocress the ecuon,
frem ene to the ether shere.

[1] Ony similority with Espronzuda is untirely coinciduntol.

SOBRE CONTRABANDO

No obstante las providencias que el gobernador ha dado contra el ilícito comercio, no ha conseguido extinguirlo porque abusan de ellas sus adláteres y confidentes, y no tiene de quien fiarse. Y se experimenta en esta ciudad y en toda la Isla una relajación absoluta en la introducción de ropas y todos géneros . . . AL REY.

Distintos almacenes venden a mercaderes y vecinos . . . AL REY.

AUN POR LAS CALLES PÚBLICAMENTE

en carretillas, por precios tan baratos como permite su adquisición en que no se pagan derechos ni se corren riesgos . . . AL REY.

Y así.

Si es que vestir pretendes con decencia,
como se viste un mariscal de Francia,
a ley ninguna prestes obediencia
y acógete a esa amable tolerancia[1]
que en todo contrabando es flor y esencia
lo mismo en Herculano que en Numancia:
Comprar mucho con poco, eso es ser ducho,
y allá quien compre poco y gaste mucho.

Bando, bando, bando,
el perrito va meando.

[1] Mejor *la tolerada tolerancia*. Pero el verso resulta largo.

ABOUT SMUGGLING

In spite of the ordinances the governor has issued to combat the illegal trade, he has not succeeded in stopping it because his trusted aides abuse the laws, and now he cannot trust anyone. And there is in this city and on the entire island a total laxness about the import of clothes and other goods . . . TO THE KING.

Certain stores sell to merchants and neighbors . . . TO THE KING.

EVEN OPENLY IN THE STREETS

in carts, at prices that are so low because there are no taxes paid to the King or any risks taken . . . TO THE KING.

And so.

If you wish to dress with elegance,
as would befit a marshal of France,
do not to any law pledge allegiance,
but follow that happy tolerance,[1]
that is the essence of all contraband,
be it in Herculaneum or Numance:
To buy much with little, that's skill, is it not,
and to let those who buy little spend a lot.

Decree, decree, decree,
The doggy goes to pee.

[1] Better the *tolerated tolerance*. But the poem is growing large.

PARÉNTESIS

Se acabó Don Juan Prado
Portocarrero;
manchado está su nombre,
roto su acero.

Los ingleses lo hallaron durmiendo a la bartola,
o por mejor decir, roncando a la española.

PARENTHESIS

Finished is Don Juan Prado
Portocarrero;
tarnished his name,
his blade is broken.

Like a sloth he was sleeping when the English came,
or better, snoring like a Spaniard without shame.

SIC TRANSIT . . .

Soneto con pequeño estrambote.

Tanta pechera y pergamino
señor Comendador qué honor
al final o a medio camino
briznas al viento no más son

Oh qué penacho peregrino
(alguien sin duda se lo dio)

*Pausa de 15
segundos a
un año*

Ahora sin penacho vino
(Quien se lo dio se lo quitó)

Se sabe que una ventolera
soplando a veces levantó
en un gran golpe a Juan Ripiera

Mas cuando el viento se aquietó
guay pergamino y guay pechera
y guay señor Comendador
qué honor.

SIC TRANSIT . . .

Sonnet with small irregularities.

All that fancy parchment and dress,
your rank, Commander, does not impress,
at the end of the road or only halfway,
dust in the wind, nothing more are they.

Oh, how fancy a plume
(someone gave it to him, we assume)

> *Pause anywhere from*
> *15 seconds to*
> *a year*

Here he comes without the plume
(they took it away, we presume)

A gust of wind, as we well know,
can at times overthrow
John the Vulgar with a single blow.

But once the wind has settled down,
gone are the parchment and fancy gown,
and gone is even the Commander,
lo and behold, what an honor.

LLANTO DE LAS HABANERAS

Esta es, señor, la fúnebre tragedia que lloramos
las habaneras fidelísimas vasallas,
cuyo poder mediante Dios rogamos
para que por la paz o por la guerra,
por tratados tal vez o por batallas
logremos el consuelo en nuestra tierra
de ver en breve tiempo aquí fijado
el pabellón de Vuestra Majestad.
Esta sola esperanza nos alienta
para no abandonar la patria y bienes,
estimando, añorando el suave yugo
del vasallaje en que nacimos.

FIN DEL LLANTO

A pesar de la pública aversión que en todas ocasiones
se manifestaba, la conducta de aquel general en el breve
tiempo de su mando fue propia de un Lord de su país.
Hubo suplicios y lástimas que deplorar que fueron in-
dispensables, porque muchos soldados ingleses habían
sido asesinados en el campo, y fuera injusto no castigar
a los homicidas.

50 negros pasados a cuchillo

figura la prisión y deportación del Obispo Pedro Agus-
tín Morell de Santa Cruz.

Puede calificarse de abusivas y tiránicas esas medidas
que a la Iglesia impuso el Conde y de atropello la orden

LAMENT OF THE WOMEN OF HAVANA

This, Sire, is the grievous tragedy that we,
the women of Havana, most faithful servants of His
    Majesty,
deplore so bitterly:
we appeal to His God-given power
that through peace or war,
through armies or treaties,
He would before long restore
the royal banner to our shore.
This sole hope gives us strength
not to abandon country and possessions at length,
praising, yearning for serfdom's gentle yoke,
under which since birth we choke.

END OF LAMENT

In spite of the public scorn felt on all occasions, the conduct of that general during the short period of his office was befitting that of a Ruler in his own country. There were tortures and cruelties to deplore, but those measures were indispensable, because many English soldiers had been murdered on the battlefield, and it would be unjust not to punish those homicides.

50 Negroes stabbed to death

there is also the imprisonment and deportation of Bishop Pedro Agustín Morell de Santa Cruz.

Can one deem abusive and tyrannical the means that the Count imposed on the Church and which outrage the religious order . . . ?

Se introdujeron algunos millares de esclavos africanos que reanimaron la agricultura.

han pedido . . . tenemos no obstante que para inde . . . su conducta se dibuje . . . con perspectiva . . . algún denigrante . . . concepto los havaneros . . . y su impericia y . . . los lances de una en

LAS MUCHACHAS DE LA HABANA
NO TIENEN TEMOR DE DIOS
Y SE VAN CON LOS INGLESES
EN LOS BOCOYES DE ARROZ

sirvió de provechosa enseñanza. En tan breve intervalo cerca de un millar de embarcaciones comerciales

Que queriendo Su Majestad evitar las cizañas que pueden ocasionar después de una Guerra las delaciones sobre infidencias, ha resuelto que ningún tribunal pueda admitirlas.

Several thousand African slaves have been imported to enliven the agriculture.

they have requested . . . we hold, however, that for inde
. . . his behavior shows . . . with perspective . . . something belittling . . . conception of the people of Havana
. . . and his lack of skill and . . . the adventures of a

THE GIRLS OF HAVANA
REALLY KNOW HOW TO BE NICE
AND JUMP WITH THE ENGLISH
INTO THE BOXES OF RICE.

It was a fruitful experience. In so brief a period, about a thousand commercial vessels entered the port.

His Majesty, wishing to avoid the evil that can occur after a War through accusations of disloyalty, has decreed that no court of law admit such accusations.

AVISO A LA POBLACIÓN

Para el 6 del presente mes de julio, en la tarde, está prevista la entrada a esta noble y siempre fiel ciudad del nuevo Capitán General Excmo. Señor Conde de Tecla. El Conde de Tecla se halla desde el 30 del pasado junio ocupando una casa de campo de estramuros de la ciudad, y en ella se preparó para la toma de posesión.

De acuerdo con lo que se sabe, la toma de posesión del Conde de Tecla comprenderá diversos actos públicos, tales como las campanas de todas las iglesias echadas a vuelo y una procesión del Ssmo. Sacramento que recorrerá en acción de gracias la extensión de la plaza de Armas, según la costumbre católica. El 7 del actual mes, el nuevo Capitán General recibirá el bastón de mando, y jurará el cumplimiento de su cargo. Se espera que Su Excelencia pronuncie un discurso congratulatorio para todos, en primer término la ciudad y Cabildo, justicia y regimiento de la Capital por su conducta durante el sitio, con la esperanza de no volver a la dominación de los herejes.

WARNING TO THE POPULATION

The solemn entry into this noble and always faithful city by the new Captain-General, His Excellency the Count of Tecla, is planned for the afternoon of the 6th of the current month of July. The Count of Tecla has been occupying a country residence just outside of the city walls since the 30th of last June, where he has prepared himself for his new office.

According to the information released, the inauguration of the Count of Tecla will involve several public acts: the bells of all churches will toll, and a procession of the Holy Sacrament will cover the whole Place of Arms as a formal act of gratitude to the Lord in keeping with Catholic custom. On the 7th of this month, the new Captain-General will receive his staff and take the oath, vowing to fulfill his duties. It is expected that His Excellency will deliver a congratulatory speech to praise especially the city justices and the regiment for their honorable behavior during the siege, so that we shall never again be overcome by heretics.

PARÉNTESIS

Paris c'est une grande ville
que también place mucho a l'espagnol.
Nous aimons les femmes françaises
y podemos decir avec Voltaire:
—Mon amie, je te compare aux cheveaux attelés
aux chars de Pharaon . . .
(Como él traduce a Salomón.)
Merci bien,
vous êtes très chic.
Salut!

PARENTHESIS

Paris c'est une grande ville
which also very much likes l'espagnol.
Nous aimons les femmes françaises
and we can say avec Voltaire:
—Mon amie, je te compare aux cheveaux attelés
aux chars de Pharaon . . .
(As he translated Solomon.)
Merci bien,
vous êtes très chic.
Health!

Luego de tan tremenda batahola
se fueron los ingleses:
Sírvese desde hoy cocido a la española,
con aliños franceses.

When the uproar came to an end,
it was the end of English rule:
From now on they serve Spanish gruel
with a French condiment.

CÓLERA

Es útil leer
lo que ha escrito del cólera morbo
Monsieur Robespierre.
Evite ese mal
por la módica suma de un real,
precio del folleto que todo lo explica
y vende el librero Palmer.

> (Ítem, en la receptoría de papel sellado a
> cargo de Don Ant⁰ de Noroña, calle de la Mu-
> ralla segunda cuadra a la derecha entrando
> por la Plaza Vieja: y estramuros en casa de
> Henri Bordeaux llamado El Francés, plazuela
> de la Salud frente al campanario viejo de
> Guadalupe.)

GANADO

Consejos y avisos a los hacendados
acerca de vacas y toros y yeguas y otros ganados:
Viniendo de Francia e instalado aquí
los da Monsieur Roche, graduado en París.

━━━━

HOTELES, FONDAS Y RESTAURANTES

Pasa a la pág. siguiente.

CHOLERA

It is useful to know
what Monsieur Robespierre had to show
about cholera's deathly blow.
You can avoid this disease
for the modest sum of a silver piece,
the price of a pamphlet explaining more,
which the bookseller Palmer has in his store.

> (Item found in don Antonio de Noroña's store
> where legal bond is sold, in the Calle de la
> Muralla, the second block on the right when
> you come from the Old Plaza: and in the out-
> skirts at the house of Henri Bordeaux, known
> as The Frenchman, Plazuela de la Salud, fac-
> ing the old Bell Tower of Guadaloupe.)

CATTLE

Advice and counsel to owners of a cattle ranch
offers Monsieur Roche who came here from France,
with a degree from Paris he knows all
about cows, bulls, mares and any other animal.

▬▬▬

HOTELS, INNS, AND RESTAURANTS

Go to the next page.

LA FLOR DE FRANCIA

GRAN FONDA DE
MADAME BOBISEUX DE BINARD
Recién llegada de París

Con posada, aunque (dicho sea con respeto) sin bidel. Cuatro reales el almuerzo y seis la comida. Servido el primero a las 8½ de la mañana y la segunda a las 3½ de la tarde. Los mejores platos en las mejores mesas; las mejores mesas en la mejor fonda. La mejor fonda, etc. Contamos con el mejor cocinero de nuestro tiempo, el mismo que alimentó durante muchos años el delicado estómago del Delfín y de S.A.R. el infante de España don Fcº de Paula (y Romero).

LA GRENOUILLE

LA RANA RESTAURANT
La Rana Restaurant
La Rana Restaurant
La Rana Restaurant   Anuncio luminiscente
La Rana Restaurant   intermitente
La Rana Restaurant
La Rana Restaurant
LA RANA RESTAURANT

THE FLOWER OF FRANCE

MADAME BOBISEUX DE BINARD'S
GREAT INN
Recently arrived from Paris

With lodging, but (if you pardon the expression) without bidets. Four *reales* for lunch and six for dinner. The former served at 8:30 a.m., the latter at 3:30 p.m. The best dishes on the best tables; the best tables in the best inn; the best inn, etc. We have the best cook of the century, the very same who, for many years, tended to the delicate stomach of the Prince and Highest Majesty, the Ruler of Spain, Don Francisco de Paula (y Romero).

LA GRENOUILLE

THE FROG RESTAURANT
The Frog Restaurant
The Frog Restaurant
The Frog Restaurant   Blinking Advertisement
The Frog Restaurant
The Frog Restaurant
THE FROG RESTAURANT

MEDICINA

BOTICA FRANCESA
Píldoras de tomate para
EL REUMATISMO

Doctor Barreiro. Real de Jesús María
(estramuros) n? 6. Especialidad en agonizantes,
desahuciados, tullidos y parturientas.
Diploma de París.

MUEBLES FRANCESES

Obispo, 101   Mad. Boibe

MADAME BARBER

En su tienda "El Tocador". Artículos franceses
exclusivamente en la Calzada de San Luis
Gonzaga al núm. 12

MADAME BUELTA

Refrescos
Paseo de Colón al comienzo.

MEDICINE

FRENCH BOUTIQUE
Tomato pills against
RHEUMATISM

Doctor Barreiro. Real de Jesús María
(outskirts), No. 6. Specializes in dying people,
cripples, hunchbacks, and recent mothers.
Diploma from Paris.

FRENCH FURNITURE

Obispo, 101   Mad. Boibe

MADAME BARBER

is at her store "The Boudoir." French imports
exclusively in the Calzada de San Luis
Gonzaga, No. 12

MADAME BUELTA

Refreshments
At the beginning of the Columbus Promenade.

LIBRERÍA: NOVEDADES FRANCESAS[1]

Dictionaire de la Musique, 2 tomos. *Histoire de France*, 1 tomo. *Oeuvres* de Molière, con preciosos grabados, 1 tomo. *Lettres* de Leoni, 1 tomo. Chopin, *Études*; los dos tomos de la *Anatomía de Bayle*; *Lettres de Mon Moulin*, de Alphonse Daudet, 1 tomo, Lamerre editeur, París; tomo V de *Les Contemplations*, de Victor Hugo con viñetas; *Études sur la Littérature et les moeurs angloméricains au XXme. siècle*, par Philarete Chasles, Paris, Amyot, rue de la Paix; *Biographie de Béranger*, Perrotin, Paris.

[1] Se ruega atentamente disimular cualquier anacronismo.

CHEZ GAMBOA

Mantecado y nevado de
frutas. Agua fría todo el año.

¡COMO EN PARÍS!

PERFUMERÍA CUBANA

Tuétano de oso y león para fortalecer el cabello. Miel de la Reina de Inglaterra, recomendada por su perfume.

EL RAMILLETE GALO

GRAN HOTEL «PANORAMA»

Contamos hasta con veinte habitaciones. Todo très chic. Quinqués y lámparas astrales en cada una.

BOOKSTORE: LATEST ARRIVALS FROM FRANCE[1]

Dictionaire de la Musique, 2 volumes. *Histoire de France,* 1 volume. *Oeuvres* by Molière, with beautiful engravings, 1 volume. *Lettres* by Leoni, 1 volume. Chopin, *Études*; the two volumes of the *Anatomía de Bayle: Lettres de Mon Moulin* by Alphonse Daudet, 1 volume, edited by Lamerre, Paris: Volume V of *Les Contemplations* by Victor Hugo, with vignettes; *Études sur la Littérature et les moeurs angloméricains au XXme. siècle,* by Philarete Chasles, Paris, Amyot, rue de la Paix; *Biographie de Béranger,* Perrotin, Paris.

[1] Politely overlook any possible anachronisms.

CHEZ GAMBOA

Ice cream and fruit ices.
Cold water all year long.

JUST LIKE IN PARIS!

CUBAN PERFUMERY

Bear and lion extracts for strengthening your hair. Queen of England honey, make it your official perfume, too.

THE GALLIC BOUQUET

GRAND HOTEL "PANORAMA"

We have up to twenty available rooms. Everything *très chic.* Oil lamps and headlamps in every room.

Terraza
parque
museo;
bosques
amor:

No hay ningún freno al deseo.
Mariposas de flor en flor.

Espacio libre y adecuado para situar quitrines y vo-
lantes del 27 de junio al 1º de setiembre. Téléphone: pas
encore. Cocina francesa.

Sierra Nubosa

Gran hotel y restaurant
francés

LE MANOIR DU LAURIER

Cocinero traído expresamente de París. Aux portes de
la capitale. Mesa redonda todas las mañanas, a las 8½.
Jamón de Westfalia. Salchichón de Hamburgo. Toci-
neta de Filadelfia. Tasajo de Cayo Romano. Plateau de
fromages.

**BAILES: DOMINGOS Y DÍAS FESTIVOS
BIDELES DE CAOBA CON VASO DE LOZA
¡AGUA ABUNDANTE!**

SANGUIJUELAS CON GUAYABA

Sanguijuelas de la Laguna
de Panda
Guayaba de Puerto del Príncipe.

«EL TRIANÓN» JUNTO A LA LONJA

Terrace
park
museum;
woods
love:

Here there are no limits to your desire.
Flutter from flower to flower like a butterfly.

Space available for carriages and coaches from 27 June
to 1 September. Telephone: *pas encore*. French cuisine.
Cloudy Mountain Range

Grand Hotel and French
Restaurant

LE MANOIR DU LAURIER

Chef especially brought from Paris. Aux portes de la
capitale. Cold buffet every morning at 8:30. Westphal-
ian ham. Large sausage from Hamburg. Philadelphia
bacon. Jerky beef from Key Romano. Assorted cheeses.

DANCING: SUNDAYS AND HOLIDAYS
OAK BIDETS WITH PORCELAIN SEATS
ABUNDANT WATER!

LEECHES WITH GUAYABA

Leeches from the Lagoon
of Panda
Guayabas from Puerto del Príncipe.

"THE TRIANON" NEXT TO THE MARKET

AGUA DE BOLLO

Obtenida del mejor maíz

«LA MARSELLESA»

ESQUINA DE MERCED Y HABANA

EL GALLO TRANSPARENTE

Gran almacén de música. Partituras (inéditas) de Beethoven. Cacharros para música sincreta, concreta y excreta

5 Ave. Oberon.

BÚSQUEDA DE UN DIRECTOR GENERAL

El grupo más importante del Cartón Ondulado (industria francesa) busca con ahinco a un director general que sea dinámico y elegante. El hombre que deseamos encontrar deberá tener más de cinco años de experiencia en el Cartón Ondulado y un año o dos de vendedor del expresado cartón. ¡¡¡Ofrecemos una situación interesante en un grupo de primer plano!!! Curriculum vitae, fotos serio y sonriente (naturaleza de la dentadura). No más de 35 años de edad. ¿Ha dirigido alguna vez un equipo de estafadores?

CARTÓN ONDULADO, S.A.

WATER OF VENUS

Made from the best corn
"LA MARSELLESA"

CORNER OF MERCED AND HAVANA

THE TRANSPARENT ROOSTER

Great music store. (Unpublished) Beethoven scores.
Utensils for syncrete, concrete, and excrete music.
No. 5, Ave. Oberon

SEARCH FOR A
GENERAL DIRECTOR

The very important group of Corrugated Cardboard
(French industries) is eagerly looking for a general di-
rector who is dynamic and elegant. The kind of person
we wish to meet must have had more than five years of
experience with Corrugated Cardboard and a year or
two of experience as seller of said product. We offer an
interesting position in a high-level business! Curricu-
lum vitae, photographs, serious and smiling (natural
teeth). No older than 35 years. Have you ever directed
a bunch of crooks before?

CORRUGATED CARDBOARD, S.A.

DICCIONARIO DE LA RIMA

Se vende un diccionario de la rima (Editorial Fallières) con una rima en *olmo* (colmo) en buen estado, y tres en *uvia* (alubia, lluvia, rubia). Se puede ver todas las tardes (hábiles) de 3 a 6. Conejos, 15. Preguntar por Inés.[1]

[1] Hemos visto este léxico. No se trata de un diccionario de la rima propiamente, sino de un diccionario normal —un PALLAS— que tiene, eso sí, uno de la rima al final de sus páginas (1485-1593).

RHYME DICTIONARY

For sale: a rhyme dictionary (Edition Fallières) with a rhyme on *olmo* (*colmo*), in good condition, and three rhymes on *uvia* (*alubia, lluvia, rubia*). Can be viewed in the afternoons (working days), from 3 to 6. Conejos, 15. Ask for Inés.[1]

[1] We have seen this lexicon. It is not a rhyme dictionary, but an ordinary dictionary—a PALLAS—which has, it is true, one of the rhymes on its final pages (1485–1593).

GRAN TEATRO TACÓN

DE PASO PARA NUEVA ORLEANS

FANNY ESSLER

Otra vez en

ESTA CIUDAD

*La conducirá a su hotel,
después de cada función
el Marqués del Carretel.*

¡Sólo ocho funciones, ocho exactamente!
A las 7 de la noche

GREAT TACON THEATER

ON HER WAY TO NEW ORLEANS

FANNY ESSLER

AGAIN

IN OUR CITY

*After each performance
the Marquis of Carretel
escorts her to her residence.*

Only eight performances, eight exactly!
At 7 p.m.

TOROS

Corrida sobresaliente y divertida en beneficio del segundo espada Juan Voltaire, torero francés. Los espectadores van a tener un rato alegre con las muertes que se ejecutarán, porque Pedro Gutiérrez dará el gran salto por encima de un toro, en otro pondrá las banderillas de nueva invención desde lo alto de un taburete, y por primera vez servirá a este digno pueblo matando el sesto toro. El Beneficiado matará el segundo toro con un par de grillos y el cual se burlará de su fiereza bailando La Cucaracha sobre una mesa al compás de la música con castañuelas.[1]

[1] El sentido de este anuncio es oscuro. Sin embargo, a nuestro parecer quiso su redactor decir que el torero, más o menos impedido de movimiento por un par de grillos, llevaría a buen término, aunque no sin riesgo y heroica temeridad, la triste muerte del indefenso animal, no que lo ultimara a grillazos. Por último hubiera sido terriblemente monstruoso que dichos grillos se los pusieran al toro.

RAPÉ, TABACO

No fume, que el tabaco da bronquitis.
El rapé lo va a hacer estornudar.
Pero si acaso el vicio lo domina
rapé y tabacos puede usted hallar:
Tabacos, en L'Etoile,
y en Obispo, rapé del especial.

Nota: Junto con el rapé adquiera por un real fuerte una botella de guarapo legítimo. De venta allí mismo.

Tabacos, Prado 77   Rapé, Obispo 41

BULLS

Outstanding and entertaining bullfight for the benefit of the second matador Juan Voltaire, a French torero. The audience will have a wonderful time with the killings to be performed, because Pedro Gutiérrez will make a great leap over a bull and stick a new kind of banderilla into another from the top of a stool; he will also, for the first time, present to this dignified audience a napping bull. The Beneficiary will kill the second bull with a pair of irons and will make fun of the animal's ferocity by dancing "La Cucaracha" on a table to the beat of the music with castanets in his hands.[1]

[1] The meaning of this advertisement is unclear. However, it seems to us that its author wishes to say that the bullfighter, more or less impeded in his movements by the pair of shackles, will kill the defenseless animal, not without risk and heroic fear but not with the irons. After all, it would be monstrous to put those irons on the bull.

SNUFF, TOBACCO

Don't smoke, because tobacco affects your throat,
while snuff will only make you sneeze.
But if the vice has got you in a squeeze,
snuff and tobacco can be got:
Tobacco in l'Etoile,
and in Obispo, snuff especial.

Note: In addition to snuff a bottle of authentic sugarcane liquor can be bought for one *real fuerte*. For sale in the same store.

Tobacco, Prado 77   Snuff, Obispo 41.

SAMBUMBIERÍA
de la
CALLE DE CUBA
Sambumbia con guaguao o sin
SIEMPRE DELICIOSA
DIRECTAMENTE DE LYON

PINTURA

Dos magníficos cuadros franceses llegados de la Coruña a esta capital. Uno representa la embriaguez de Lot por sus hijas, y el otro la cena de Baltasar, rey de Babilonia. Dicen los artistas y personas de buen gusto que son obras de mérito extraordinario por su antigüedad y perfección. Se hallan a la expectación pública en la sala de la imprenta del «Noticioso y Lucero».

Nada place a un alma pura
como la buena pintura.

JACQUES DUPONT

Por dos onzas de oro, un retrato al óleo; en miniatura, 30 pesos y medio. Con manos, precios convencionales, sea con una, sea con las dos. A escoger: parecido absoluto o parecido relativo, en ambos casos con la misma perfecta maestría.

PAINTING

Two magnificent French paintings have arrived in the
capital from Coruña. One depicts Lot's daughters get-
ting him drunk and the other the supper of Balthasar,
King of Babylon. Artists and people with good taste
consider these works of extraordinary merit because of
their age and perfection. They are exhibited for the
public in the ballroom of the press "Noticioso y
Lucero."

Nothing pleases a pure soul more
than a good painting to adore.

JACQUES DUPONT

Oil portraits for 2 ounces of gold; miniatures for 30½
pesos. Conventional prices, with hands, either one hand
or two. Your choice: total or partial likeness, in each
case with the same degree of perfection.

JEAN CONDILLAC

Pintor francés sin brazos. Se le considera mucho más hábil que el célebre M. Nellis.

EL SEÑOR FERRI

Retratista al óleo y pintor de casas. Precios módicos.

AYER EN EL PUERTO

Entraron los siguientes barcos de cabotaje cuya carga se relaciona más abajo, con sus nombres y el de sus patronos: guairo «San Simón», de Cárdenas, su patrón Hernández, con 400 sacos de carbón.

Goleta «Pilar», de Canímar, su patrón López, con 500 sacos de carbón.

Balandra «La Empresa», su patrón Carlos, con 800 sacos de carbón, de La Siguapa. Trajo también 40 caballos de leña.

Goleta «Teresa», de Cabañas, su patrón Romero, con 107 cajas de azúcar y 4 pipas de aguardiente.

Ninguno encontró mal tiempo en su derrota, salvo el pequeño ciclón que dañó la arboladura del «San Simón». El mismo fenómeno estuvo a punto de ocasionar la pérdida de la goleta «Teresa».

JEAN CONDILLAC

French painter without arms. Reputed to be much more gifted than the renowned M. Nellis.

SEÑOR FERRI

Paints oil portraits and houses. Modest prices.

YESTERDAY IN THE HARBOR

The following coastal clippers entered the harbor. Their cargo, as well as their names and those of their captains, are listed below: the clipper *San Simón* from Cárdenas, Captain Hernández, with 400 sacks of coal.

The schooner *Pilar* from Canímar, Captain López, with 500 sacks of coal.

The sailing boat *La Empresa*, Captain Carlos, with 800 sacks of coal from Siguapa. It also carried 40 horse loads of firewood.

The schooner *Teresa* from Cabañas, Captain Romero, with 107 bags of sugar and 4 barrels of cane liquor.

None of them encountered bad weather during the course of their respective voyages, with the exception of a small hurricane that damaged the masts of the *San Simón*. The same storm almost caused the loss of the schooner *Teresa*.

Salió para Burdeos la fragata francesa «Paquebot Bordelais», pasaje y carge general. Para el mismo destino, el hermoso bergantín francés «Louis Philippe».

Para Nueva York, la acreditada fragata francesa «Martha». Muy segura, forrada y claveteada toda de bre.

EL «FIDO»

Se encuentra anclado en bahía (en cuarentena) el bergantín americano «Fido», procedente de Salem. Su cargamento: harina de maíz, manteca, mantequilla, arenques ahumados, lenguas de bacalao, cebollas, velas de esperma. Dicho barco trae la suma de 1600 onzas de oro consignadas a los señores Mariátegui y C°, de esta plaza, y un catre.

DESGRACIA

La Gaceta del Gobierno de Matanzas, cuyo último número llegó ayer a nuestra ciudad, nos da cuenta de lo que sigue:

Trinidad, 8 de junio.—La flechera Guarda-costa Fernandina y goleta mercante española Esperanza, en su navegación de Batabanó á este puerto, hallándose en la mañana del 4 del corriente como a cosa de 23 millas al Sur de la boca de Jágua, encontraron zozobrada una goleta de velacho al parecer americana, y habiendo procedido á su reconocimiento con la lancha, opinaron ser muy reciente la desgracia; la arboladura y velamen tendido en el agua en orden de navegar; parte de la maniobra picada;

The French frigate *Paquebot Bordelais* left for Bordeaux with passengers and general freight. The beautiful French brigantine *Louis Philippe* sailed for the same destination.

The accredited French frigate *Martha* sailed to New York. Very safe, well provisioned, and nailed completely with copper.

THE FIDO

The American brigantine *Fido*, coming from Salem, is anchored in the bay (under quarantine). Her cargo consists of corn meal, lard, butter, smoked herring, slices of codfish, onions, wax candles. Said vessel carries a total of 1,600 ounces in gold for Mariátegui and Co., of this city, and a bed.

MISFORTUNE

The Gazette of the Government of Matanzas, whose latest issue arrived in our city yesterday, informs us about the following:

Trinidad, June 8th.—During their voyage from Batabanó to this port, the Coast Guard vessel *Fernandina* and the Spanish commercial schooner *Esperanza*, finding themselves about 23 miles south of the mouth of the Jágua on the morning of the 4th of this month, happened on a capsized sailing ship that looked American. Upon further exploring the vessel from a boat, they had reason to believe that the misfortune had been a recent one. The masts and the sails were lying in the

la popa más sumergida que la parte de proa; cuyo motivo impidió que se pudiera leer el nombre del buque; el cargamento de maderas; el casco negro y pendol verde; la lancha trincada y desfondada, observándose que en los trancaniles se notaban algunos manchones de sangre; de suerte que no hallándose a nadie en el buque ni en todo lo que se alcanzaba á la vista y repararse al rededor reunión de tintoreras han creído que pudo haber sufrido algún hecho de piratería.

La comandancia de Marina ha recibido el correspondiente parte del de la Flechera. Los patrones D. Estéban Coraza y Luis González, han informado que el día 2 salieron ámbos de Jágua: que la goleta americana Charles of Philadelphia, su capitán Coquin, debía verificarlo también para Philadelphia con cargamento de maderas, pero que no lo efectuó aquel día por falta de viento que tal vez lo haría al día siguiente 3. Añaden que el casco y pendol tienen los colores que se han indicado; de manera que hasta ahora

water, part of the ship's body was pierced; the stern was more under water than the prow, which made it impossible for them to read the name of the vessel; the cargo was wood; her body was black and the bottom green. The ship was torn apart and bottomless. They also found large bloodstains on the planks. Not finding anybody in the boat or in sight, and also noticing a gathering of sharks, they believed that the ship had been the victim of pirates.

The commander of the Coast Guard received a corresponding report. The shipmasters Don Estéban Coraza and Luis González have informed us that both had left Jágua on the 2nd of this month and that the American schooner *Charles of Philadelphia*, with Captain Conquin, had planned on sailing for Philadelphia that very day with a load of wood but could not because there was no wind; and that perhaps she had sailed on the following day, the third. They add that the ship's hull was of the color mentioned above; in such a way that until now

COOLIES

LEGÍTIMOS DE MACAO

Tan buenos como negros
y
más económicos

INFORMES:
DON DOMINGO DE ALDAMA

Agente general en toda la Isla.

AUTHENTIC COOLIES

FROM MACAO

As good as Negroes
and
more economical

INFORMATION:
DON DOMINGO DE ALDAMA

General Agent for the whole Island.

CARPINTERO DE VIEJO

Se reparan vírgenes

Todos los días (excepto los domingos) al lado de la catedral.

FUNERARIAS

El cadáver es suyo. El entierro es nuestro. El resto sólo es de Dios.

FUNERARIA LITERARIA DE LUJO «CARONTE»

Caronte & Hijo

La preferida por el gran mundo.

REPAIRMAN FOR OLD THINGS

Virgins restored.

Every day (except Sundays) next to the cathedral.

FUNERALS

The body is yours. The burial is ours. The rest is up to God.

LITERARY AND LUXURIOUS FUNERAL HOME "CHARON"

Charon and Son

Preferred by high society.

GRAN FUNERARIA «BERCEO»

Si en tu mortal momento,
te viene al pensamiento
la idea de escoger sitio adecuado
para ser enterrado,
pide a tus familiares
que le hablen por favor a Blas Casares.
Él tiene separado
(claro, no por capricho),
un nicho para ti, que es, más que nicho,
logar cobdiciaduero para ome cansado.[1]

Nuestro lema:

NO LUJO, COMODIDAD PARA EL DIFUNTO

[1] Sin alarde ninguno de erudición, que está lejos de nuestro ánimo en estos solemnes momentos, hacemos constar que esta cita es de Gonzalo de Berceo en su introducción al célebre poema *Los Milagros de Nuestra Señora*, 8º verso. Edición D.T.A. Sánchez, Paris, BAUDRY-Librería Europea. 1842.

GREAT FUNERAL HOME "BERCEO"

If your final hour is near
and your mind is troubled by the fear
that a fitting place be selected
where your final rest is protected,
then please make your family agree
that Blas Casares is the man to see.
He has prepared for you a spot
that is a lot more than just a lot,
(not whimsically, you bet)
a desirable place for your weary head.[1]

Our motto:

NOT LUXURY, BUT COMFORT FOR THE DECEASED

[1] Without boasting of erudition, which is far from our mind in those solemn moments, we wish to note that this quotation is from Gonzalo de Berceo's introduction to the famous poem *The Miracles of Our Lady*, 8th verse. Edition D. T. A. Sanchez, Paris, BAUDRY—European Bookstore, 1842.

PARÉNTESIS

Primero fue de esta manera:
En un lugar de octubre
Céspedes encendió su profunda bandera.
El clarín resonaba.
Ay, por diez años
aquel clarín resonaría.
Todo pasó de madrugada,
y nunca fue la madrugada día.

PARENTHESIS

In the beginning it was this way:
In October, one night
Céspedes' banner burned bright.
The bugle called,
and for ten years, alas,
that sound would not pass.
Early one morning it happened this way,
and never would dawn become day.

GOBIERNO Y CAPITANÍA GENERAL
DE LA SIEMPRE FIEL
ISLA DE CUBA

Turbado el orden público en algunas localidades del departamento oriental de esta isla, pretendiendo trastornar insurreccional y violentamente la manera social de existir de los honrados habitantes de Cuba, que con laboriosidad y a la sombra de la nacionalidad española la han sabido conducir al grado envidiable de prosperidad en que se encuentra, he considerado como el primero y más alto de mis deberes acudir enérgicamente al restablecimiento de la paz, y con este objeto e dispuesto ocupar militarmente el territorio perturbado, adoptando cuantas medidas conducen al fin que franca y lealmente manifesté en mi alocución del día 11 del corriente, y que pronto serán confirmadas por el gobierno supremo; y siendo congruente a este propósito robustecer la acción firme, eficaz y pronta de la Autoridad Pública, para que el castigo de los que puedan desoir la voz de su deber sea tan ejemplar y ejecutivo como las circunstancias exigen, no siendo éstas sin embargo de tal gravedad que demanden la necesidad de un estado general de excepción que pueda lastimar intereses respetables, y aun preocupar el ánimo de los habitantes leales, cuya tranquilidad, sosiego y libertad precisamente me propongo proteger y asegurar: usando de las facultades que me conceden las leyes vigentes, y con particularidad el Real Decreto de 26 de noviembre de 1867, vengo a decretar lo siguiente:

THE GOVERNMENT AND CAPTAINCY-GENERAL OF THE ALWAYS LOYAL ISLAND OF CUBA

As in some parts of the eastern province of this island the public order has been disturbed by the attempt to overturn, through revolution and violence, the way of life that the honorable citizens of Cuba, through hard work and under the protection of the Spanish government, have turned into its present enviable state of prosperity, I have considered it the first and highest of my duties to reestablish the peace rigorously. For this reason I have ordered military occupation of the troubled territories and have adopted several measures to achieve such a goal, which are spelled out frankly and loyally in the speech I gave on the 11th of the current month, measures soon to be ratified by the highest courts. This proposition calls for firm, efficient, and immediate action on the part of the Public Authorities, because circumstances demand that the punishment of those who turn a deaf ear to the call of duty be carried out in an exemplary manner. But those circumstances are not so serious as to demand a general state of martial law that would inconvenience the interests of respectable citizens, and even preoccupy the minds of the loyal citizens, whose tranquillity, peace and liberty are precisely what I intend to protect and ensure: With the authority vested in me by current legislation, and particularly the Royal Decree of 26 November 1867, I ordain the following:

ARTÍCULO PRIMERO. Las comisiones militares establecidas por mi decreto del 4 de enero último, conocerán también desde hoy, con exclusión de toda jurisdicción y fuero, de los delitos de rebelión, traición y sedición.

ARTÍCULO SEGUNDO. Quedan en consecuencia sujetos al juicio y fallo de dichas comisiones todos los que se alzaren públicamente para destruir la integridad nacional; los que con cualquier pretexto se rebelasen contra el gobierno y las autoridades constituidas, o trastornasen de algún modo el orden público; los que redacten, impriman o circulen escritos o noticias subversivas; los que interrumpan las comunicaciones telegráficas; los que detengan o intercepten la correspondencia pública, los que destruyan las vías férreas o pongan obstáculos en los demás caminos públicos para proteger a los revoltosos, los conspiradores o auxiliadores, en fin, de todos estos delitos, sus cómplices y encubridores.

ARTÍCULO TERCERO. En la tramitación de las causas se observarán los términos breves y perentorios marcados en las ordenanzas del Ejército, y en la designación de las penas, las leyes comunes del Reino que rigen en esta provincia.

ARTÍCULO CUARTO. Lo dispuesto en los artículos anteriores no deroga ni modifica los bandos que hayan dictado o dictasen en uso de sus facultades propias o delegadas de mi Autoridad Superior los Gobernadores Militares de los distritos en que la rebelión se ha manifestado o manifestare, a los jefes de las fuerzas que operan en ellas.

FIRST ARTICLE. As of today, the military courts established through my decree of last June 4th will hear the cases of those accused of the crimes of rebellion, treason, and sedition, to the exclusion of all jurisdictional limits and exemptions by law or territory.

SECOND ARTICLE. Consequently, all those who rise in public revolt to destroy the nation's integrity; who, for whatever reason, rebel against the government and the established authorities, or in any way disrupt public order; who author, print, or circulate subversive writings or notices; who interrupt telegraphic communication; who detain mail or disrupt the postal services; who destroy railroad tracks or obstruct other public thoroughfares to protect the revolutionaries, the conspirators and their accomplices or anybody who helps them cover up their operations; all those are subject to the jurisdiction of said tribunals.

THIRD ARTICLE. The hearing of these cases will follow the swift and summary procedures of military law, while the penalties will be determined according to the common law of the Kingdom that rules this province.

FOURTH ARTICLE. The above articles do not invalidate or change decrees that have been or will be issued by the superior authority of the military governors in the districts where the rebellion has been or is taking place, dispatched by the leaders of the forces stationed there.

ARTÍCULO QUINTO. Estas disposiciones cesarán por medio de una disposición oficial que se publicará en la Gaceta tan pronto como cesen los motivos que me han obligado a dictarlas. Habana, 20 de octubre de 1868. EL CAPITÁN GENERAL, Francisco Lersundi.

FIFTH ARTICLE. These orders will be superseded by an official decree that will be published in the Paper as soon as the reasons that have forced me to impose these orders have ceased to exist. Havana, 20 October 1868. THE CAPTAIN-GENERAL, Francisco Lersundi.

ANÁLISIS CRÍTICO HISTÓRICO Y FILOSÓFICO

de la

GUERRA LLAMADA DE LOS DIEZ AÑOS

DEBIDO A UN GRUPO DE ESCRITORES CUBANOS, CON EL TEXTO DEL PACTO DEL ZANJÓN Y TODO LO RELATIVO A LA PROTESTA DE BARAGUÁ

SEPARE SU EJEMPLAR CON TIEMPO

CRITICAL, HISTORICAL, AND
PHILOSOPHICAL ANALYSIS

of the

SO-CALLED TEN-YEARS
WAR

BY A GROUP OF CUBAN WRITERS
WITH THE TEXT OF THE PACT OF
ZANJÓN AND ALL THAT IS
RELATED TO THE PROTEST OF BARAGUÁ

RESERVE YOUR COPY IN TIME

ÚLTIMAS NOVEDADES EN LIBROS CUBANOS

RAFAEL MARÍA MENDIVE. Poesías corregidas y notablemente aumentadas. Prólogo de don Manuel Cañete, académico, y una biografía de D. Vidal Morales, $2.50.

LANDALUCE. Tipos y costumbres de la Isla de Cuba. Esta obra ha sido redactada en colaboración con los mejores escritores e ilustrada con veinte láminas de Landaluce. Un volumen en folio, $8.00.

ENRIQUE JOSÉ VARONA. Conferencias filosóficas, primera serie. Un volumen 4º menor, rústica, $1.50.

ARPAS AMIGAS. Colección de Poesiás por los señores Sellén, Varona, Borrero, Tejera, Betancourt y Varela.

ANTONIO LÓPEZ PRIETO. Parnaso cubano, desde Sequeira hasta nuestros días. Un volumen, 4º, $4.50.

TODAS ESTAS OBRAS HAN SIDO EDITADAS POR LA LIBRERÍA NACIONAL Y EXTRANJERA DE MIGUEL VILLA, CALLE DEL OBISPO Nº 160, HABANA.

LATEST NOVELTIES
IN CUBAN BOOKS

RAFAEL MARÍA MENDIVE. Poetry, revised and considerably enlarged edition. Prologue by Don Manuel Cañete, scholar, and a biographical sketch by Don Vidal Morales. $2.50.

LANDALUZE. Types and Customs of the Island of Cuba. This work has been produced in collaboration with the best writers and is illustrated with twenty engravings by Landaluze. One volume, folio, $8.00.

ENRIQUE JOSÉ VARONA. Philosophical Lectures, first series. One volume, quarto, soft cover, $1.50.

FRIENDLY LYRES. Collection of poetry by Sellén, Varona, Borrero, Tejera, Betancourt, and Varela.

ANTONIO LÓPEZ PRIETO. Cuban Parnassus, from Sequeira until today. One volume, quarto, $4.50.

THESE WORKS HAVE BEEN PUBLISHED BY THE NATIONAL AND FOREIGN LIBRARY OF MIGUEL VILLA, OBISPO STREET No. 160, HAVANA.

PARÉNTESIS

Luego pasó de esta manera:
diversa y ella misma flotaba la bandera.
El clarín otra vez, y ya era día.
Luego pasó de esta manera:
El cielo azul se abrió rasgado
por la uña extranjera.
Espeso inglés de maquinaria
el rostro de la patria detenía.

PARENTHESIS

And then it happened this way:
the banner was different yet the same.
The bugle again, and then daylight came.
And then it happened this way:
A large foreign fingernail
tore open the skies.
Thick English of machineries
turned the nation's face to ice.

Las últimas noticias que hemos publicado dan por hecho el desembarco del cabecilla Maceo en la playa de Duaba . . .

El ánimo por otra parte se sorprende ante la consideración de que un Guillermón, un Maceo, un Crombet se erijan en paladines de un país cuya cultura los rechaza.

El país ha protestado con magnífica
unanimidad contra
el crimen separatista . . . La
nación, con la serenidad de su misericordia,
ofreció el perdón a los arrepentidos.

LLENA DE NOBLEZA EN SU JUSTICIA SÓLO FIRMARÁ ESTA VEZ LA PAZ CON LA PUNTA DE LAS BAYONETAS

LA GUERRA TIENE UN CARÁCTER RACISTA UN CARÁCTER RACISTA UN CARÁCTER RACISTA UN CARÁCTER RACISTA UN CARÁCTER RACISTA UN UNA SUICIDA INTENTONA CUBA RECHAZA LA GUERRA —COSAS DE LOCOS QUE NO DEBEN ANDAR SUELTOS— UN PUEBLO DIGNO QUE BUSCA SU BIENESTAR. NOTICIAS.

. . . The last news we published considered a fact the
landing of the outlaw rebel leader Maceo on the beach
of Duaha . . .

> *The soul, on the other hand, was struck by the
> idea that a Guillermón, a Maceo, a Crombet
> would emerge as defenders of a country
> whose culture rejects them.*

The country has protested with magnificent
unanimity against
the crime of separatism . . . The
nation, with serene mercy,
granted pardon to those who repented.

FILLED WITH RIGHTEOUS NOBILITY, IT WILL ONLY SIGN THE PEACE WITH THE TIPS OF BAYONETS

THE WAR HAS A
RACIST CHARACTER
RACIST CHARACTER
RACIST CHARACTER
RACIST CHARACTER

AN ATTEMPT AT SUICIDE
CUBA REJECTS THE
WAR—ACTS OF LUNA-
TICS WHO SHOULD NOT
BE ON THE LOOSE—A
DIGNIFIED PEOPLE
CONCERNED WITH ITS
WELL-BEING. NEWS.

. . . pues los demás jefes de la pasada guerra, que como es sabido son muchos en aquella provincia, no sólo no han tomado parte en el movimiento, sino que lo rechazan, agregando que de los sublevados las siete octavas partes pertenecen a la raza de color.

Ha caído Martí, la cabeza pensante y delirante de la revolución cubana

La muerte de Maceo ha sido plenamente confirmada

PIE DE GRABADO

El general Calixto García y el general Ludlow (norteamericano) conferencian después del desembarco de las tropas yanquis. *Foto Ignotus.*

CUBA NO FUE ADMITIDA A LA CONFERENCIA DE PARÍS, A PESAR DE HABER PELEADO POR SU INDEPENDENCIA DURANTE MÁS DE MEDIO SIGLO

(Cintillo a 8 columnas) 1ª

Manifestaciones populares en toda la Isla contra la Enmienda Platt.

Ultimátum de Estados Unidos a Cuba: Enmienda o nada.

NUESTRA PROTESTA

(Editorial)

. . . for the rest of the leaders of the last war, who are, as is known, numerous in that province, have not only not taken part in the movement but reject it outright, adding that ⅞ of the rebels belong to the colored race.

Martí killed, he was the thinking, delirious head of the Cuban Revolution

Maceo's death has been overwhelmingly confirmed

INSCRIPTION BELOW A PHOTOGRAPH

The generals Calixto García and Ludlow (North American) meet after the landing of the Yankee troops. *Photograph: Unknown.*

CUBA HAS NOT BEEN ADMITTED TO THE PARIS PEACE CONFERENCE, DESPITE HAVING FOUGHT FOR HER INDEPENDENCE FOR MORE THAN HALF A CENTURY
(8 columns) page I

Public protests against the Platt amendment throughout the Island.

United States ultimatum to Cuba: Amendment or nothing.

OUR PROTEST

(Editorial)

ANUNCIAMOS LA INMEDIATA
APARICIÓN
DE UN ESTUDIO
COMPLETO DE LA GUERRA HISPANO
CUBANA AMERICANA
CON SUS CAUSAS, DESARROLLO E
INTERVENCIÓN DEL GOBIERNO DE
ESTADOS UNIDOS EN ELLA
TAMBIÉN EL TEXTO COMPLETO DEL
TRATADO DE PARÍS A CUYA FIRMA NO
FUE INVITADA CUBA
Y EL DE LA ENMIENDA PLATT ASÍ COMO
LA PONENCIA EN CONTRA REDACTADA
POR EL SEÑOR JUAN GUALBERTO
GÓMEZ DELEGADO A LA ASAMBLEA
CONSTITUYENTE

LLAMAZARES Y COMPAÑÍA
LIBREROS IMPRESORES. HABANA

ANNOUNCING THE IMMEDIATE
PUBLICATION
OF A COMPLETE STUDY
OF THE SPANISH CUBAN
AMERICAN WAR
WITH ITS CAUSES, DEVELOPMENT, AND
THE INTERVENTION OF THE
GOVERNMENT OF THE UNITED STATES
ALSO INCLUDES THE COMPLETE TEXT
OF THE PARIS TREATY TO THE
SIGNING OF WHICH CUBA WAS NOT
INVITED AND OF THE
PLATT AMENDMENT AS WELL AS
THE COUNTERSTATEMENT BY JUAN
GUALBERTO GÓMEZ, DELEGATE TO
THE CONSTITUTIONAL ASSEMBLY

LLAMAZARES AND COMPANY
Printed Books, Havana

CURIOSIDADES

En la vitrina del diario «Centro de la Marina», se halla expuesto a la curiosidad pública el artístico machete que una comisión de veteranos de la independencia de Cuba regaló al general Leonard Wood el 20 de mayo último con motivo de la instalación de la república. El arma reposa en un magnífico estuche fabricado con las más preciosas maderas del país. Según se dice, el general ha correspondido gentilmente al hermoso gesto de los veteranos obsequiándolos a su vez con un ejemplar de la Enmienda Platt, encuadernado, y en cuya tapa frontal figura un grabado que representa el águila norteamericana con las alas abiertas en toda su envergadura.

EL REY DE LA SUAVIDAD

Dadme, oh Musas, el cándido deleite
de cantar al aceite
que llaman "Essolube",
en el techo subido de una nube.
La Standard soberana,
que procesa este oil,
lo brinda a la república cubana.
HIGHER AND HIGHER EVERY DAY
      Standard Oil Co.

CURIOSITIES

In the window of the newspaper Centro de la Marina, *there is on public display the dress sword that a group of veterans of the Cuban War of Independence presented to General Leonard Wood on last May 20th at the inauguration of the republic. The weapon rests in a magnificent box made of the country's most precious woods. It is rumored that the general has responded kindly to this beautiful gesture on the part of the veterans, presenting them in return with a bound copy of the Platt amendment whose front cover is embossed with the North American eagle with his wings spread wide.*

THE KING OF SMOOTHNESS

Grant me, oh Muse, the simple pleasure
of singing to that oily treasure
by the name of "Essolube,"
from a cloud's lofty altitude.
The Standard so majestic,
which processes this oil,
toasts with it to the Cuban republic.
HIGHER AND HIGHER EVERY DAY
            Standard Oil Co.

SNACK BAR

Perros calientes. Perras en la misma situación.
Pida «Mompox» (aguardiente). Tomado poco a poco
ayuda a una perfecta digestión. Menú: $2.20.
Ave. de la Conflautación.   Self service.
El pan a discreción

UNA OBRA QUE HARÁ ÉPOCA

Querido señor o señora:

Invitamos a usted oficialmente a facilitarnos los datos
sobre su persona, que se incluirán en el presente mo-
delo, destinados a la confección de un nuevo diccion-
ario biográfico de un prestigio y de una calidad excep-
cionales, a saber:

WHO'S NOT

Su colaboración será altamente apreciada por todos los
interesados. ¡Veinte mil hombres y mujeres famosos y
eminentes presentados con elegancia insuperable en un
solo volumen!

AUTOS, TRACTORES Y CAMIONES FORD

FORD NO ES UNA PALABRA, ES UNA INSTITUCIÓN

SNACK BAR

Hot dogs. Bitches in the same condition.
Ask for Mompox (cane brandy). Sipped slowly, it will
do wonders for your digestion. Menu: $2.20.
Breadloaf Avenue.   Self-service.
Choice of bread

AN EPOCH-MAKING WORK

Ladies and Gentlemen:

We officially invite you to provide us with your personal
data by filling out the enclosed questionnaire, for the
purpose of compiling a new biographical dictionary of
exceptional prestige and quality, entitled:

WHO'S NOT

Your cooperation will be much appreciated by all who
have an interest in this project. Twenty thousand fa-
mous and eminent men and women included in a single
volume of insuperable elegance!

CARS, TRACTORS, AND FORD TRUCKS

FORD IS NOT A WORD, IT IS
AN INSTITUTION

RESERVADO PARA LA GRAN CARNICERÍA
«THE STAR»

El propietario, el administrador y los
empleados todos de la panadería «The Bread»
desean a usted unas felices Pascuas
y un Año Nuevo tan
próspero como
venturoso

SUSCRÍBASE A NUESTRO DAILY Y ESTARÁ
UP TO DATE

EL AÑO PRÓXIMO, LA SERIE MUNDIAL COM-
PLETE DESDE NUESTRAS PÁGINAS. —CADA
MATCH INNING POR INNING TRASMITIDOS
DIRECTAMENTE DESDE NEW YORK POR PIPI
Y PAPÁ.

REMITIDO

Joven inquieto, desearía correspondencia con alguna
joven de 18 años hasta 30.
Garantizo ÉXITO. La alegría y las ideas modernas de-
ben ser nuestro lema. Un poco atronado, pero
RESPONDO.
Tengo los ojos rubios and el pelo verde. ¡Por favor!

RESERVED FOR THE GREAT MEAT MARKET
"THE STAR"

The owner, the manager, and the
staff of the bakery "The Bread"
wish you a Merry Christmas
and a happy and
prosperous New Year.

SUBSCRIBE TO OUR *DAILY* AND BE
UP TO DATE

NEXT YEAR, THE COMPLETE WORLD SE-
RIES WILL BE COVERED IN OUR PAGES. —
EACH *MATCH, INNING* BY *INNING*, RE-
PORTED DIRECTLY FROM NEW YORK BY PIPI
Y PAPÁ.

CORRESPONDENCE

Restless young man wishes to correspond with a young
woman, 18 to 30 years old.
SUCCESS guaranteed. Pleasure and modern ideas
must be our theme. A bit crazy, but RESPONSIVE.
I have blond eyes and green hair. Please!

SYRGOSOL

No espere a que su enfermedad secreta se haga
   pública

SANITUBE

Visite a Venus sin temer a Mercurio. El preventivo
oficial del ejército norteamericano. En todas las
farmacias

YA . . . YO . . . YA . . .

Pruebe las píldoras vitalinas, y cambiará de opinión.
También la cambiarán sobre usted.

PRESERVATIVOS

de piel de majá. Cómodos. Resistentes. Durables.
Elegantes.

DINERO EN HIPOTECA

Préstamos en todas cantidades sobre fincas rústicas y
urbanas. Interés no más del 20% diario.
THE NATIONAL BANK. Reserva absoluta.

SYRGOSOL

Do not let your secret illness become public

SANITUBE

Visit Venus without fearing Mercury. The official prophylactic of the North American army. Available in all pharmacies.

YA . . . YO . . . YA . . .

Try vitamin pills, and change your mind. People will also change theirs about you.

CONDOMS

made of snake skin. Comfortable. Resistant. Durable. Elegant.

CASH FOR MORTGAGES

We lend any amount on real estate in the country and in the city. Interest no more than 20 percent daily. THE NATIONAL BANK. Absolute discretion.

MIAMI CLUB

Diviértase cada noche bailando con las mejores orquestas de la Habana. Estrictamente privado. Clientela distinguida en su mayoría norteamericana. Aviso importante: la Administración o su delegado a la entrada del local se reservan el derecho de admisión, sin explicaciones. Buffet frío y platos criollos. Show especial a las 12, con la negra Rufina y el negrito Cocoliso, los mejores bailadores de la rumba cubana.

NO PASE APUROS

Si es usted empleado, goce de la vida, no sufra las angustias de fin de mes. Pregunte por Chicho, calle de las Palmas, accesoria del 9, frente a la barbería. Reserva absoluta.

TRANSPORTE

¡Viaje en tren!

Polines o traviesas de majagua, ácana, granadillo, jiquí, ébano real, para las líneas de nuestros ferrocarriles. Los mejores árboles y finas maderas al servicio de la seguridad y elegancia ferroviaria nacional. Bosques hasta que se acaben.

THE CUBAN RAILROAD COMPANY

Havana   Cuba

MIAMI CLUB

Have fun every night dancing to the best orchestras of Havana. Strictly private. Distinguished clientele, mostly North Americans. Important notice: the Management or its representative at the gate to the premises reserves the right to deny admission, without explanations. Cold buffet and creole dishes. Special show at 12, with the Negress Rufina and the little Negro Cocoliso, the best performers of the Cuban rumba.

DON'T BE PRESSED

If you have a job, enjoy life, do not suffer from anguish at the end of the month. Ask for Chicho, Street of the Palm Trees, Accessory 9, opposite the barbershop. Absolute discretion.

TRANSPORT

Go by train!

Beams and crossbeams made of majagua, ácana, granadillo, jiquí, royal ebony, for the tracks of our railroad carriages. The best trees and the finest woods for the security and elegance of the national railroads. Forests until they last.

THE CUBAN RAILROAD COMPANY

Havana   Cuba

FÁBULA

Recorriendo un labrador
sus campos una mañana,
(Termina en la página 4)

TIPERRITA

Se ofrece como mecanógrafa señorita cubana de buena familia, educada en Boston, USA. Ardiente como un crisol de la cabeza a los pies. Habla muy bien el inglés y no mal el español. En esta imprenta informarán.

DOMÉSTICA

Se busca una muchacha para atender a un niño de dos años. Si no es blanca, o mestiza adelantada, que no se presente. Calle X N° 60[1]

---

[1] No hemos podido encontrar la calle X en el Vedado, por lo que suponemos que ya no existe. Pero existió sin duda antes de la Revolución.

FABLE

One morning a peasant
returned to his fields,

(Concluded on page 4)

TYPIST

Cuban girl from good family, educated in Boston, USA,
is seeking employment as a stenographer. Hot like a
cauldron. Speaks English very well. Her Spanish is not
bad either. Information available at the press.

HELP WANTED

Nanny for two-year-old boy. Applicants need not in-
quire unless they are white or light-skinned mulattoes.
Street X, No. 60.[1]

---

[1] We have been unable to locate Street X in Vedado; we therefore
presume that it does not exist. But it no doubt existed before the
Revolution.

MAQUINARIA

De máquinas en todo lo sabido,
todo lo averiguado,
nadie jamás ha visto así reunido
un stock tan variado
y en realidad tan poco conocido.

PURDY AND HENDERSON

son, cual siempre fueron,
los toros en el ramo que escogieron.

LA METROPOLITANA

MACHINERY

About machines we know all,
we check everything out;
no one has ever seen en bloc
such a variegated stock
that we really know very little about.

PURDY AND HENDERSON

are, and always have been,
the bullies of any business they're in.

THE METROPOLITAN

Vote por los liberales en estas
elecciones

Sin Libertad no hay
Progreso

TIBURÓN SE LO DARÁ

LIBORIO:

Ya sea gente pobre o gente rica,
todos copian de un mismo refranero:
Se baña el tiburón, pero salpica;
ahí viene el mayoral sonando el cuero.

Vote por los conservadores en estas
elecciones
Sin orden no hay
Libertad

EL MAYORAL SE LA DARÁ

LIBORIO:

Ahí viene el mayoral sonando el cuero.
Se baña el tiburón, pero salpica.
Todos copian de un mismo refranero
ya sea gente pobre o gente rica.

Vote for the Liberals in these
elections

Without Freedom there is no
Progress

SHARK WILL PROVIDE IT

LIBORIO:

All people, be they rich or poor,
have the same proverbs in store:
The shark swims well, but he splashes.
The overseer doles out whiplashes.

Vote for the Conservatives in these
elections
Without Order there is no
Freedom

THE OVERSEER WILL PROVIDE IT

LIBORIO:

The overseer doles out whiplashes.
The shark swims well, but he splashes.
All have the same proverbs in store,
be they rich or be they poor.

ALELUYAS

Por siempre alabado sea
El licor puro de Brea.

Lo inventó el Dr. González
Hace treinta años cabales.

Su fama con fuerza vibre
Por tierra de Cuba libre.

Para los males del pecho
Es lo mejor que se ha hecho.

Al viejo que tose fuerte
Lo cura y libra de muerte.

La vieja que sufre asma
Al mejorar se entusiasma.

Señora, no se haga sorda,
Pruébelo y verá si engorda.

Balsámico y vegetal,
No reconoce rival.

Cura bronquios y garganta
Y los catarros espanta.

De BREA tiene el LICOR
Un agradable sabor.

Se vende cosa tan rica
De SAN JOSÉ en la BOTICA.

Todo el mundo la conoce
En HABANA ciento doce.

HALLELUJAHS

Forever be praised, wide and far
The clear liquid made from Tar.
Dr. González invented it
thirty years ago, to wit.
His fame vigorously resonates
Throughout the free Cuban states.
For disease of the chest
It is by far the best.
The old man who's choking,
It keeps him from croaking.
The old woman who's asthmatic,
Gets better and ecstatic.
Madam, don't turn a deaf ear,
Try it and see how plump you'll appear.
Soothing and wholly vegetal,
It has absolutely no rival.
It cures bronchitis and throat pain
And scares colds down the drain.
It's TAR that makes this BEVERAGE
More flavorful than average.
This liquid from SAN JOSÉ is unique
And sold in the BOUTIQUE.
Everyone knows it
At 112 Havana Street.

DECÁLOGO

Por Enrique Lluvi

Si te agrada ser liberal, no hay problemas: puedes seguir siendo conservador.

No vendas tu voto, pero si lo vendes, trata de amarrarte a una buena nómina. Tú sabes que no hace falta trabajar.

Rechaza las ideologías extranjeras. Los comunistas son enemigos de los liberales y de los conservadores. También están contra la Enmienda Platt.

Recuerda que cada capitán de policía es un pozo sin fondo. Los hay malos, pero también los hay peores. En problemas de charadas, bolita o de alguna protegida tuya, úntalos en forma. No te pesará.

El día de las elecciones habla gordo cuando sea necesario, pero ni una gota de sangre. Después del escrutinio, el mismísimo 2, ya tú sabes cómo es el elemento: si te he visto, no me acuerdo. Las experiencias abundan.

Trata de ir a todos los velorios, bautizos, matrimonios que haya en tu barrio, y por supuesto en tu cuadra. Si te crees con facultades para ello, en case de entierro despide el duelo. Pero entérate antes de la edad del difunto: algunos no pasan de seis meses.

Especialízate en las licencias de armas, para lo cual debes cultivar la amistad del jefe del negociado correspondiente. Sobre todo que la primera licencia sea la tuya. Evita el 45. Es preferible siempre el Colt 38.

DECALOGUE

By Enrique Lluvi

If you like being a liberal, no problem: you can continue being conservative.

Do not sell your vote, but if you do, try to hang onto a good payroll. You know you don't really have to work.

Distrust foreign ideologies. The Communists are the enemies of the liberals and the conservatives. They are also against the Platt amendment.

Remember that each police chief is a bottomless pit. There are bad ones, but there are also some who are worse. If you have a problem with them about the numbers or a female friend, just lay a little dough on them. You will not regret it.

On election day, talk big, if necessary, but don't spill any of your own blood. After the elections, you already know the ropes: if I have seen you before, I won't remember it. These things happen a lot.

Try to attend all the funerals, baptisms, and weddings in your district and of course on your block. If you have a talent for this, deliver the eulogy at the funeral. But before that find out the age of the deceased; some are not even six weeks old.

Specialize in gun licenses, in which case you will have to cultivate the friendship of the head of the appropriate office. Above all, let the first license be yours. Avoid the .45. The .38 Colt is always preferable.

No uses coco-macaco, que ha perdido mucho prestigio. Si crees útil un bastón, cómprate uno de estoque y riega al voz. No tendrás nunca que valerte de él porque la gente lo respeta.

Cuando NO HAGAS un favor, no te lo atribuyas; ni tampoco ¡esomenos!, cuando lo hagas. Di siempre que es cosa de tu jefe, que tú no hiciste más que cumplir sus órdenes, que el jefe fue quíen te mandó, etc. Trata de que el jefe sepa que tú procedes así.

Todos estos consejos, mandamientos o como quieras llamarlos, se resumen en uno solo: EL JAMÓN ES SAGRADO. Cuanto trabajes por obtenerlo, aunque sea en lascas o ya en el hueso, tiene la más absoluta justificación de la cátedra. Sin embargo, actúa con elegancia. (*Comunicado*).

DE ADMINISTRACIÓN

Se recuerda una vez más al público en general que todos los textos destinados a publicarse en esta sección están sujetos a la tarifa correspondiente. Los trabajos que pudieran prestarse a confusión, llevarán al final la palabra «comunicado».

Do not use coco-macaco, which has lost much of its prestige. If you find a cane useful, buy one that has a long narrow sword inside and spread the word. You will never have to use it because people respect it a lot.

If you don't do a favor, do not attribute it to yourself; even if you do, don't do that either. Always say that it was your boss who did it, that you have done nothing more than comply with his orders, and that your boss was the one who ordered you to do it, etc. Make it known to your boss that you act this way.

All these pieces of advice, commandments or whatever you wish to call them, amount to one thing: THE GRAFT IS SACRED. No matter how hard you work to get it, even if you only get it in slices or just the bone, everything you do is justified by the experts. But do it in style.
(*Press Release*)

ABOUT THE ADMINISTRATION

The general public is once more reminded that all texts to be published in this section are subject to the appropriate fee. Those pieces which might cause confusion will be followed by the phrase "Press Release."

NOTAS DE SOCIEDAD

Por Fradique Fontanals

«On dit . . .»

Una gentil trigueñita, residente en el aristocrático «faubourg» vedadense, ha sido alcanzada por la dulce flecha de Cupido.

¿Nombre? Imposible.

Nos está prohibido.

No sólo por la más elemental discreción, sino porque el compromiso no es todavía formal.

Sólo sus iniciales.

Que son T. S. H.

Las cuales recuerdan un sistema de lo más inalámbrico de trasmitir noticias.

Tampoco diremos el nombre del afortunado galán, «pitcher» suplente de un afamado «team» de «baseball».

He aquí sus iniciales: P.A.U.

Las mismas de un partido gubernamental que hace unos meses pasó a mejor vida.

Pronto despejaremos la incógnita . . .
Nada más, sino que nos sentimos «enchantés», como decía el famoso Baudelaire.

SOCIETY NEWS

By Fradique Fontanals

"On dit . . ."

A graceful brunette, resident of the aristocratic "faubourg" of Vedado, has been pierced by Cupid's sweet dart.

Name? Impossible.

We do not have permission.

Not only because of the most basic discretion but also because the engagement has not yet been formalized.

Only her initials.

Which are T. S. H.

They remind one of a wireless communication system.

Nor can we reveal the name of the lucky groom, substitute "pitcher" for a famous "baseball team."

Here are his initials: P. A. U.

They are the same as those of a government party that lost power a few months ago.

We will soon lift the veil of this mystery . . .
Enough, but we are "enchantés," as the famous Baudelaire put it.

Hacia el ultramarino pueblo de Regla, de donde seguirán viaje rumbo a la villa de Pepe Antonio, partieron ayer dos «girls» que son el encanto de sus respetabilísimos padres, el acaudalado banquero Don Sinecuro de la Pampa Rescoldo y su señora esposa Doña Minesota T. Frío de la Pampa Rescoldo.

Numerosas amistades acudieron a despedirlas.
En la siempre concurrida y cosmopolita Esquina de Toyo. La estancia de las deliciosas «jeunes-filles» será brevísima. «Bon voyage».

—oOo—

Todavía resuena en nuestros oídos el eco de tan brillante fiesta.

Una noche de «charme», como decía Verlaine.
Era de esperar, tratándose de la opulenta familia Siguanea.

Que desde hace varios años ha establecido su residencia en nuestra turbulenta «city».

Con general beneplácito.

Fue la boda de Cusita, la monísima hija mayor de los esposos Siguanea, que contrajo quintas nupcias, esta vez con el correcto joven Walter Rice Taylor y Pimienta, de la mejor sociedad del Histórico Cayo, como llamamos cariñosamente a Cayo Hueso.

Bajo una iluminación «a giorno», que hacía resaltar sus naturales encantos, se presentó la novia.

Yesterday, two "girls" who are the pride of their very respectable parents, the acclaimed banker Don Sinecuro de la Pampa Rescoldo and his wife Doña Minesota T. Frío de la Pampa Rescoldo, departed for the overseas city of Regla, from where they will continue their journey to the town of Pepe Antonio.

Countless friends came to bid them farewell.
At the always busy and cosmopolitan Esquina de Toyo.
The stay of the delicious "jeunes-filles" will be brief.
"Bon voyage."

———oOo———

Today our ears are filled with the echo of a most brilliant party.

A night of "charme," as Verlaine used to say.
It was to be expected, since the event was sponsored by the opulent family Siguanea.

They became residents of our turbulent "cité" several years ago.

Much to everyone's pleasure.

It was the wedding of Cusita, the cute oldest daughter of the couple Siguanea, who married for the fifth time, this time the proper young gentleman Walter Rice Taylor y Pimienta, of the best circles of the historical Key, as they tenderly call Key West.

The bride was presented under lights "a giorno," which brought out her natural charm.

Vestida iba con un hermoso traje de «moaré», de color verde-nilo-desmayado.

El velo amarillo huevo (nos referimos a la yema) caía como un sutil niágara de seda sobre las ebúrneas espaldas de la gentil «fiancée».

Tanto el vestido —elegantísimo— como el velo, debidos fueron a las manos del modisto del momento.

Tito Tato, el gran «desinateur» femenino.

Que se ha anotado un triunfo más.

El joven Walter, naturalmente emocionado, iba del brazo de la feliz mamá, la señora de Siguanea.

Vestía un elegante «smoking» cortado por el simpático Juancho Rizoto, el sastre de los que están a la moda.

La novia, resplandeciente en su delicadísima virginidad, daba el brazo a su señor padre, Don Sinecuro.

Párrafo aparte.

Para el adorno floral de la elegante mansión donde se celebró el fastuoso enlace.

Que es la de los padres de la novia.

Una obra maestra del mundialmente famoso jardín «El Repollo» de los hermanos Lechuguetes.

El ramo de la boda, confeccionado fue por otro jardín, mundialmente célebre también.

She was wearing a beautiful gown of "moiré," whose color was a faint Nile green.

The egg-yellow veil (we are of course referring to the yolk) fell like a subtle silken niagara over the chalk-white shoulders of the graceful "fiancée."

The entire outfit, like the veil very elegant, must have been composed by the most fashionable designer of the day.

Tito Tato, the great "desinateur" of women's fashions.

He has scored another victory.

Young Walter, naturally overcome with emotion, took the arm of the happy mama, Mrs. Siguanea.

He wore an elegant "smoking," made by the well-liked Juancho Rizoto, the tailor for those who go with the times.

The bride, aglow with the splendor of her very delicate virginity, extended her arm to her father, Don Sinecuro.

New paragraph.

The sumptuous wedding was celebrated in an elegant mansion adorned with flowers.

Which belongs to the bride's parents.

The masterful work of the world-famous garden shop "El Repollo" owned by the brothers Lechuguete.

The wedding bouquet was provided by another gardener, also world famous.

No citaremos su nombre, sin embargo, en virtud de una orden expresa de nuestro Administrador, siempre tan correcto.

Leída que fue la Epístola de San Pablo a los distinguidos contrayentes, la feliz pareja partió hacia Miami, donde pasará la luna de miel.

Pero la fiesta prosiguió, entre oleadas de «champagne», rubio y espumoso, de la acreditadísima marca «Poison», que representa con exclusividad para toda la República nuestro particular amigo Rufo Raffo.

Delicadísimo el siempre bien afinado conjunto del maestro Roncesvalles.

Infaltable en las reuniones de la «high-life».

Nuestros votos.

Consignados sean con toda sinceridad.

Por la ventura eterna de los ya felices esposos, que han visto coronados sus dulces sueños «d'amour».

Y un pronto regreso a nuestra «ville», donde se verán de nuevo agasajados por los numerosos miembros de su «entourage».

Como decía Montesquieu.

——oOo——

Ayer recibió las regeneradoras aguas del Jordán, el robusto e inteligente niño Jamelgo Peplo —como quedó

We will, however, not give its name, in compliance with a strict order from our Manager, who is always so right.

After the Epistle of Saint Paul had been read to the distinguished couple, the happy newlyweds left for Miami where they will spend their honeymoon.

But the party continued amid waves of "champagne," blond and foamy, of the accredited brand "Poison," sold in our Republic exclusively by our special friend Rufo Raffo.

Very delicate as always was the well-tuned music played by a band under the leadership of Maestro Roncesvalles.

Never absent from the parties of the "high-life."

Our best wishes.

May they be received with all sincerity.

To the eternal happiness of the already happy couple, whose sweet dreams "d'amour" have become reality.

And a quick return to our "ville," where they will again be feted by the numerous members of their "entourage."

As Montesquieu used to say.

———oOo———

Yesterday the robust, intelligent boy Jamelgo Peplo, the fourteenth "enfant" of the indefatigable marriage of

consagrado— décimo cuarto «enfant» del infatigable matrimonio formado por Doña Insistencia de las Mercedes Rejo y Don Resignado Peplo.

Con tan simpático motivo, se sirvió en casa de los esposos Peplo Rejo un magnífico «buffet», procedente del ya clásico restaurant-cafetería «La Mesa».
¡Felicidades, «petit ami»!

———oOo———

Nota de duelo.

Ha dejado de existir, confortado por los auxilios de la Santa Madre Iglesia Católica Apostólica Romana y después de recibir la Bendición Papal, el correcto, honorable y generoso «gentleman» Don Aparicio Pasonte, Marqués del Cheque, que de tanta simpatía gozó siempre en nuestra mejor «societé».

Según es sabido, Don Apa, como afectuosamente llamábamos al Marqués sus amigos, sufrió un agudo ataque de traidora enfermedad, que le afectó el cerebro, con motivo de las últimas distribuciones terráqueas y en lo tocante a los tradicionales y siempre bien recibidos préstamos con interés.

Que en él era bajo, como es de todos conocido.

Esto le captó numerosas simpatías entre los funcionarios de distintos Ministerios, donde también ha sido lamentadísima su temprana desaparición.

Mañana, a las 9 a.m., tendrá efecto el acto de su sepelio.

the Doña Insistencia de las Mercedes Rejo and don Resignado Peplo, received the holy waters of the Jordan.

A magnificent buffet was served on this occasion in the house of the couple Peplo Rejo which was catered by the already classic restaurant/cafeteria "La Mesa." Congratulations, "petit ami"!

———oOo———

Condolences

The proper, honorable, and generous "gentleman" Don Aparicio Pasonte, Marquis del Cheque, who has always been held in amiable esteem by the best circles of our "societé," has passed away, comforted with the help of the Apostolic Roman Catholic Church of the Holy Mother and after having received the Papal Benediction.

As is known, Don Apa, as his friends affectionately called the Marquis, was suffering from a massive attack of a treacherous illness that affected his brain, this being a result of the latest land distributions and the traditional and always well-received loans with interest.

Which, as all know, was low in his case.

his earned him many friendships among the bureaucrats of several state departments, where his untimely passing has also been lamented.

The funeral will be held tomorrow at 9 a.m.

Tanto el tendido como la conducción del cadáver al lugar de su eterno descanso, correrán a cargo de la acreditada funeraria «La Preferida».

Hasta la inconsolable viuda de Don Aparicio y todos los familiares del extinto, especialmente su hijo Aparicito, dueño de la magnífica farmacia «La Aspirina», hacemos llegar nuestro más sentido pésame.

Descanse en paz, como decía Walter Johnson.

All the necessary preparations as well as the transport of the body to the site of his eternal rest will be arranged by the accredited funeral home "La Preferida."

We extend our deeply felt condolences to Don Aparicio's inconsolable widow and all the relatives of the deceased, especially his son Aparicito, owner of the magnificent pharmacy "La Aspirina."

Rest in peace, as Walter Johnson used to say.

JEFATURA DE LA POLICÍA NACIONAL

Se hace saber:

Que con motivo de la visita a La Habana del Hon. Calvino Cooleriche, presidente de los Estados Unidos de América, queda terminantemente prohibida cualquier demostración hostil al ilustre huésped, gran amigo de Cuba, así como toda alusión a la Enmienda Platt, a la Estación Naval de Guantánamo, a la zafra azucarera o en general a las inversiones de ciudadanos de Estados Unidos en nuestro país. Estos hechos se considerarán atentatorios no sólo a las reglas de la más elemental cortesía y buena vecindad, sino a las relaciones amistosas que tradicionalmente han existido entre nuestra pequeña isla y el coloso del Norte, e implicarán penas de multa o de prisión, o ambas a la vez.

Fernández y Compañía - Rodríguez y Compañía - Martínez y Compañía - Álvarez y Compañía - González y Compañía - Gutiérrez y Compañía Angones y Compañía - Tamames (perdón) y
    Compañía

CALLE DE LA MURALLA:
EL WALL STREET ESPAÑOL

Presidente Cuban   Diputado Cane
Generales Sugar   Oradores Sugar
Senadores Cane   Millonarios Cuban

CUBAN SUGAR CANE

NATIONAL POLICE HEADQUARTERS

To be announced:

Because of the visit to Havana by the Honorable Cal-
vino Cooleriche, President of the United States of
America, all demonstrations of hostility to our illus-
trious guest, the great friend of Cuba, are strictly pro-
hibited, as well as any allusions to the Platt amend-
ment, the Guantánamo Naval Base, the sugar crop, or,
in general, to the investments of United States citizens
in our country. Such acts will be considered offensive
not only to the most elementary rules of courtesy and
good neighborliness but also to the friendly relations
that have traditionally existed between our little island
and the colossus of the North and will carry a penalty
of fines or jail, or both.

Fernández and Company—Rodríguez and
  Company—
Martínez and Company—Álvarez and Company
González and Company—Gutiérrez and Company
Angones and Company—Tamames (excuse me) and
  Company

CALLE DE LA MURALLA:
THE SPANISH WALL STREET

President Cuban	Deputy Cane
Generals Sugar	Orators Sugar
Senators Cane	Cuban Millionaires

CUBAN SUGAR CANE

LA QUINCALLA DEL ÑATO agujas de coser y de máquina papalotes bolas de cáñamo para los mismos alfileres de cabecita alfileres de criandera botones cintas de variado ancho chancletas de palo para el baño frazados de piso cepillo y pasta de dientes chicles chambelonas brillantina sólida y líquida hilo blanco y de color salfumán y creoline perfumes de siete potencias flores de papel mejores que las legítimas postales iluminadas sellos de correos peinetas tijeritas peines antina para zapatos blancos esponjas grandes y pequeñas torticas de Morón serpentinas y confetis esmalte de uñas ojetes palos de trapear oraciones entre ellas la de San Luis Beltrán para el mal de ojo la de San Judas Tadeo la del Justo Juez bombillas eléctricas velitas de Santa Teresa la oración del Ánima Sola redecillas para el pelo calcetines masa real crocante de maní y ajonjolí caballitos de queque encajes y broderíes agujas de tejer estropajo de aluminio y de pita talco hebillas para cinturones y para el pelo papel de carta y sobres calcomanías lápices Mikado cordones de zapatos blancos y amarillos betún almohadillas de canevá cartilla de la última edición libro de cuentos para colorear pachulí coladores de café y de leche papel para trabajos manuales puntos de pluma caretas y antifaces papel secante papel crepé papel higiénico papel de lija elásticos de todos los anchos bloomers y ajustadores aceite de máquina tres en uno calzoncillos y camisetas flit clavos tornillos y tuercas puntillas tira flechas acuarelas abanicos pencas chinas y de guano poleas para máquinas de coser polvo jabones de olor bolitas de vidrio monederos aretes collares agua florida de Cananga cinta de hiladillo pulsos prendedores filarmónicas sortijas chinelas carátulas tiza blanca y de color pomos de tinta de escribir negra azul y morada barajas españolas y ameri-

THE 100 PERCENT DISCOUNT STORE

needles for sewing and sewing machines kites string for those kites pins safety pins buttons ribbons of various widths wooden clogs for the bath mops toothbrushes and toothpaste chewing gum lollipops hair grease paste and liquid white fabric disinfectant perfumes of seven potencies paper flowers better than the real ones picture postcards stamps decorative combs scissors combs white shoe polish large and small sponges little Moran pancakes streamers and confetti nail polish mop handles snap buttons prayers including the one to San Luis Beltrán against the evil eye the one to San Judas Tadeo the one to the Just Judge light bulbs Santa Teresa candles Ánima Sola prayers hair nets socks real peanut and sesame mass little cake horses lace and embroidery knitting needles scouring pads made of aluminum and agave threads talcum powder belt buckles and berets stationery and stickers Mikado pencils white and yellow shoelaces shoe polish little pillows reading boards coloring books fragrances strainers for coffee and milk construction paper for cutting and pasting pen nibs masks small and large blotters crepe paper toilet tissue sandpaper suspenders of various kinds panties and bras machine oil "Three in One" men's shorts and undershirts insecticide nails screws bolts and nuts slingshots watercolors Chinese fans straw fans and palm leaf fans belts for sewing machines powder bath soaps marbles wallets earrings necklaces afterbath splash from Cananga woven ribbons bracelets pins harmonicas rings slippers cardboard white and colored chalk ink bottles black blue and purple Spanish and American decks of cards lockets powder boxes lipsticks thimbles calendars eyebrow pencils zippers glue small black-

canas dijes moteras creyones de labios dedales alma-
naques creyones para las cejas zippers goma de pegar
y de borrar pizarritas juegos de yaquis brochas y na-
vajitas de afeitar palitos de tendedera billetes de lotería
piedras para fosforeras boquillas de hueso para cigar-
ros palillos de dientes pelotas de goma trompos piedra
imán con limalla.

boards jacks brushes and razor blades clothespins lottery tickets flints cigar holders made of bone toothpicks rubber balls tops magnets with iron shavings.

TEATRO REPUBLICANO

RESUMEN NACIONAL

con la opereta de gran

espectáculo

LAS HIJAS DE ELENA
ERAN MÁS DE TRES

O

DE LEONARDO A GERARDO

Pasando por Paso Franco

ENTRADA GRATIS — SALIDA A

TROMPADAS,

TROMPETAS Y TROMPETILLAS

La Habana, 1933.

REPUBLICAN THEATER

NATIONAL OPENING

of the spectacular

operetta

HELEN'S DAUGHTERS
WERE MORE THAN THREE

OR

FROM LEONARDO TO GERARDO

Passing by Paso Franco

FREE ADMISSION—EXIT

WITH A BANG,

TRUMPETS AND EAR TRUMPETS

Havana, 1933

U.S.A. ES LA ESPERANZA DE CUBA- TODOS UNIDOS BAJO LA BANDERA DE U.S.A.

Fragmento:

> . . . Por lo demás, espero que recuerdes
> aquella tempestad que hubo de risas
> cuando de blancas que eran las camisas
> se convirtieron en camisas verdes.

SIN AZÚCAR NO HAY PAÍS - DULCE PARA TODOS Y TODOS PARA EL DULCE

Fragmento:

> ¿Y por qué no decirlo? —repetía
> floja la voz y la dicción cansada.
> Pasó un día y un día y otro día,
> y por fin el doctor no dijo nada.

BATISTAFIO

Cuba, fértil provincia y señalada
en la de cáncer luz maravillosa;
por su dulzor de caña respetada
y por fuerte, serena y poderosa:
Como sin ti, señora, el todo es nada,
o al menos viene a ser muy poca cosa,
el general (¡salud!) que todo era,
a ser nada volvió como cualquiera.[1]

---

[1] Cualquier parecido o identidad de estos versos con los de otros poetas (así sea el poderoso Don Alonso de Ercilla, o nuestro Plácido) es pura coincidencia.

U.S.A. IS CUBA'S HOPE—ALL UNITED UNDER THE FLAG OF THE U.S.A.

Fragment:

> . . . Moreover, I hope you remember
> the outburst of laughter
> when formerly white shirts
> turned drab green hereafter.

WITHOUT SUGAR THERE IS NO COUNTRY—SWEET FOR ALL AND ALL FOR THE SWEET STUFF

Fragment:

> And why not say it?—I would again say,
> diction slurred, voice breaking.
> A day went by, yet another day,
> in which Dr. Grau had nothing to say.

BATISTAPH

Cuba, fertile province of such greatness,
you bathe in the cancer's marvelous light,
respected for your sugarcane's sweetness
and for your strength, serenity, and might.
For without you, Lady, the whole is worth nothing,
or its worth would at least be very slight,
the General (salut!) who once was everything,
has become nothing again overnight.[1]

---

[1]Any resemblance or identity of these lines to those of other poets
(perhaps the powerful Don Alonso de Ercilla or our own Plácido) is
purely fortuitous.

28 DE ENERO

DESFILE POPULAR Y
GRAN ACTO
DE MASAS

A LAS 9 DE LA NOCHE

¡ASISTA!   ¡ASISTA!

Sepa cómo impedir a tiempo, con la independencia de Cuba, que se extiendan por las Antillas los Estados Unidos y caigan con esa fuerza más sobre nuestras tierras de América.

HABLARÁ JOSÉ MARTÍ

28th OF JANUARY

PUBLIC PARADE AND GREAT
DEMONSTRATION
OF THE MASSES

AT 9 O'CLOCK TONIGHT

BE THERE!   BE THERE!

Learn through Cuba's independence how
to prevent in time the United States from
taking over the Antilles and from forcibly
subjecting to their rule our countries in the
Americas.

JOSÉ MARTÍ WILL SPEAK

AVISO

Acaba de aparecer «La Historia me absolverá». Un volumen en cuarto, artísticamente impreso, con fotos y documentos inéditos.

HAY UN EJEMPLAR PARA USTED

Editorial Moncada.

ANNOUNCEMENT

The text of "History Will Absolve Me" has just appeared. One quarto volume, artistically printed, with photographs and unpublished documents.

THERE IS A COPY FOR YOU

Moncada Publications

FINAL

Luego pasó de esta manera:
Su gran frente sombría
sintió arder el Turquino.
La sangre en rudas oleadas vino
a tocar a la puerta de otro día.
Luego pasó de esta manera:
Céspedes sonreía.
Flotaba la bandera.
Alta y sola flotar se la veía.

Todo fue así, de esa manera.

FINALE

Then it happened this way:
Turquino's great, somber forehead
was flushed with fiery red.
Harsh waves of blood galore
would pound at the new day's door.
Then it happened this way:
Céspedes smiled contently.
The flag flapped merrily.
It was flying high and solitary.

It was all like this, exactly this way.

Compositor: Wilsted & Taylor
Text: 12/14 Bauer Bodoni
Display: Bauer Bodoni